THE CHILD BRIDE
(no one knew my pain)
A TRUE STORY

THE CHILD BRIDE
(no one knew my pain)
A TRUE STORY

Written By:

Mary F Smith

ISBN: 1-58820-987-3

This book is printed on acid free paper.

EDITORS:
CORRINE BRANCH
BERYL BENNETT
DEBRA HALL

1stBooks – rev. 3/26/01

DEDICATION

This book is dedicated to my four beautiful children, Tefa, Lil' James, Lil' Mary and D'Angelo. I pray that some day each of you will gain the courage to read this book and get to know me for who I really am rather than who or what I was portrayed to be. I pray we can continue the bond we have grown to share through much pain and frustration. May God enhance our unconditional love.

And to my sisters, Janice, Clara, Banita, Sharlette and Fran, in spite of our differences, you were everything I'd hoped to be. Most of all, to my dearest mother who was and is always my hero!

Table Of Contents

Preface

I had considered writing this book years ago, especially in the days I would sit alone in my bedroom crying wondering how I was going to go on, or how long would I have to endure a marriage that was forced upon me at the age of 14. Now I can see why I didn't pursue it then. It wasn't the right time. Now that the time has come, I want to say this book is not written out of revenge or anger, but as a way of healing, therapy, and growth for me. I hope my story will encourage and uplift the women and young girls with a similar situation, and perhaps motivate them to tell their own unique life story. May God teach, instruct and inspire you through every chapter.

TO THE READER

I pray you can read this book with an open heart and mind. In certain life situations, people have different opinions and views. We must remember that we are not the same. What may work for some does not necessarily work for others. Someone can advise you, but no one has the right to make a decision for you that will affect the rest of your life. If you are not meeting their expectations, this can produce guilt feelings. It is very difficult to handle this burden. If you're totally irresponsible or incapable of making wise or sensible decisions, then you have only yourself to blame.

Perhaps you're wondering where I'm coming from, I speak from the perspective of a child bride. In the United States, people have the freedom to choose a spouse; there are instances where this right has been taken away from us and the decision made by others who have authority over us. Do the church, parents, or ministers have a right to make that decision for you? Does God actually give them the authority to tell you whom you are to marry? I understand the value of advice and counsel in assisting those we love in making the right choice. It is written in the scriptures; "In the multitude of counsellors there is safety". (Proverbs 11:14) But how far can one go in counseling of others? Are there guidelines to be followed?

Foreword

I have been in ministry over 50 years, and over a period of time I've had the opportunity to embrace many lives from various walks of life. As I traveled over the country I've had the inexplicable pleasure of witnessing God's movement in great capacities within this ministry that He has placed in my charge. For out of this ministry have come great miracles of healing, restorations and other ministries. With great pleasure I introduce to you another one of God's unique vessels whom I believe God has raised up for this day and time. Over the years there have been many that has been a part of this ministry, but I must admit this young woman is one of a kind. I can remember the first time she walked into my office for counseling. As I listened to this then, broken vessel, I wept as I began to share with her some of the things God had brought me through. From the moment God allowed her to become a part of the Monument of Faith Church, she has been an asset to this ministry. Every time she would mount the platform along with the Voices of Monument singing, "Nobody Like Jesus" you can feel the presence of the anointing of God, as the congregation would join in all over the building. There was no other way to say it accept; I'm glad to have her as a part of this ministry.

This young woman has an extraordinary testimony that you are about to share. With in the pages of this book is one of the most exceptional stories that I had been privileged to read. It reveals a situation that's prevalent yet hidden in our churches today. Society of certain cultures accepts it as a way of life. Up until now no one has dared to question or challenge it. Upon sharing her testimony I understood why God allowed Bishop Jakes to preach "Woman Thou Art Loose". Well here's one of those women that God has loosed from life's traumatic experiences. I must say I strongly believe God has raised up this vessel to bring another rim of healing, deliverance and freedom to his people. You have got to read this book, and once you've read it I declare "You will never be the same.!"

Apostle Richard D Henton

Monument of Faith, Chicago

A Silent Turmoil

I never had that southern mentality where women were reared to be bread bakers and baby makers. I've always felt a woman should be able to enjoy her marriage as much as the man.

We are not human mattresses, having to spread every time he wants to spill. But the coming together of man and woman as husband and wife should be enjoyable for both individuals, not a one-sided responsibility. My heart goes out to every little girl in foreign countries and in the South that has had to endure such trauma. No one knows the effect this selfishness has on the mind and spirit except those who had actually lived through the experience. Whether it was because of tradition, cultural, or religious beliefs, I refuse to believe that all of the children who were put in those circumstances went quietly like a sheep led to the slaughter. Some, like me, were forbidden to speak out, so either out of fear or obedience they submitted.

I realize times have changed, but can you identify with me for a moment? During my childhood days, the most a 14-year old girl knew about sex was through something they heard from peers or read in a pulp magazine. Perhaps they had been raped or molested. As for those who were blessed to remain virgins: to have their innocence taken away through an arranged marriage doesn't erase the shame and humiliation they feel as they submit unto the act with no feelings of love or respect. Just a feeling of responsibility to a man who is in many cases much older than they are.

As quiet as it is kept, if the situation is not handled properly, no matter how these young girls appear outwardly, inwardly they become resentful and bitter. There is no greater turmoil then children whose made to endure such evasion of their minds and emotions. Yet, they must remain SILENT!

The Author

INTRODUCTION

MEMORIES

There are so many memories crowded in my head. I pray I can put them in order to the best of my ability.

I was born in a little suburban town in the city of Chicago, the ninth child of ten children. I was brought up in a decent home with my Mom, Dad, four brothers and five sisters.

My family and I lived in a neighborhood where every house on the block was similar, except for a few minor differences. Some had the awnings with a large initial imprinted on top, representing the last name of the family that lived there. Others had various types of aluminum sidings. Overall, they were basically brick front, frame side homes, consisting of four bedrooms, living room, dining room, kitchen, and bathroom. Some of the neighbors who had fewer children could afford to have their fourth bedroom transformed into a dining room. This was middle class living in a south suburban African American neighborhood.

Having a family of ten children, Mama had arranged the two back bedrooms with twin beds in each. One was the girls' room where my sisters, Fran, Sharlette, Janice, Banita, and I slept. The other room was for my four brothers, Lonnie, Charles, Carlton and Ryan. There was another bedroom down the hall across from the bathroom. Mama gave that room to Clara, since she was the oldest child. Clara was more like the second mother. She was mama whenever Mama was away from home.

Mama and Dad had the front bedroom located next to the living room. Being the knee-baby, the second youngest, I had the privilege of choosing where I slept. Sometimes I slept with Mama, Clara, or my other sisters. Most times I slept with Clara. She was my favorite.

When I was born, my family was moving economically from a lower class to a middle class family. Mama and Dad had purchased their first new home in Robbins, Illinois, a few years before they had their last two children, Banita and me. My family had lived several places prior to buying their own home, including staying with other relatives. Now we were blessed with more material advantages. We didn't have a lot of extra money, but we were taught well how to take little and make it enough to go around. Many days Mama had to pray and ask God to provide a meal, not knowing how or where it was going to come from, just knowing God was able.

Those were my grooming days, preparing me for life and all of its pitfalls. This was the times of struggle when we had nothing but faith in the refrigerator and prayer in the living room. This implanted a deep trust in God in our hearts. There was no other way. Mama was not one that accepted handouts. Not once did I ever hear her complain during our times of need. We were taught to endure those times in life. No matter how hungry we were, we could neither beg nor accept what was offered.

I can remember the times we would visit other peoples' homes and they would offer us something to eat. We would look at Mama see a certain look in her eyes; then we would humbly say, "No, thank you" with a smile. On the inside at times we were dying to say "Yes." But like Mama, we must be strong. I'm more than grateful to say we made it through those times and things began to get better.

There was a bright side in the midst of those times. My family was very gifted with musical talents. Clara played the piano and the organ. Lonnie played the guitar and drums. And all of the rest of us could sing. If we couldn't lead, then Mama taught us how to sing background in perfect harmony.

Mama was the cream of the crop. She was a beautiful woman: caramel brown complexion, five-feet, four inches tall, medium built, with a head full of long thick black hair. Mom was where the talent began. Mom was not only a singer; she could play the piano with great skill. Mom had a piano in the living room someone had given her. The wood was dull and scratched and a few of the keys were sticking, but Mom played as if she had a brand new Baldwin. Many days, through the hard times, Mom would gather everyone into the living room around that little brown wooden piano to sing praises to God.

I loved singing. Every time my turn came to sing I would belt out notes with no shame, be they in the right or wrong key. I treasured singing the gospel. Even as a child it gave me such fulfillment. I was too young to sing with the family group. But every time they would rehearse, I would sit up on the back of the couch in the living room and imagine how it was going to be when my time came.

I would imagine my singing on another level. To me, my purpose for singing was not just because I could sing. I wanted to sing with a special anointing where people could get healed, delivered, and set free just by hearing me. In those days I was inspired by Reverend Gene Martin, a renowned gospel singer of that time, from Miracle Valley, Arizona. When the Miracle Valley Magazine would come to our house, Gene Martin was often featured in an article telling how people received deliverance just by hearing him sing. God, I wanted that! Yes! That was priceless.

Other than Gene, Mama was my main inspiration, especially in singing the gospel. I've never heard anyone, other than Aretha Franklin, sing "Amazing Grace" like Mama did. Every time Mama would sing that song, it would bring tears to my eyes. Whenever she would sing it at church I would be on the edge of my seat hollering, "yes: Sing it Mama!" I was her greatest fan.

But our visions clashed when it came to the possibilities of spreading the gospel through song on a greater level. I wanted us to be able to sing world wide, to record, and to travel. To me, the sky was the limit. If those in the secular world could do it, why couldn't we? Why was gospel music limited to the church?

Mama didn't believe God wanted us to become recording artists. It was all right to do an independent project, but to get caught up in the music industry was not of God. She felt it would cause us to stray. Well, I felt that since we were saved, surely if God could save us, He could keep us. As much as we loved God, surely we wouldn't stray, especially singing gospel music. But I could only push so far Mama's word was law. In those days you didn't question the advice or opinion of the parents or any other adult; the answer was always, "because I said so." No matter what, they always knew what was best, and they were always right.

I wasn't the only one in the family that had a vision for singing gospel music. My eldest brother, Lonnie, felt the same way. Lonnie wrote, played, and sang gospel music. He also envisioned recording and traveling. But again Mama said this was not the will of God. Our purpose was to sing in the church and whenever we traveled with the ministry. God would not be pleased with anything more.

Nevertheless, Lonnie was persistent. He knew there was more; he wanted to use the talents and abilities God had granted him to their fullest capacity. Therefore, he persisted in his request to Mama to at least let him participate in gospel concerts. Finally Mama consented.

Lonnie formed his own group and began to sing in every concert available throughout the city of Chicago and occasionally in other cities and states. Later on he started singing with my sisters and me. I had been waiting for that opportunity. It not only gave me a chance to express my talent and passion for gospel music, but I had the privilege of singing in concerts with artists such as Milton Brunson and The Thompson Community Singers, Jesse Dixon, Inez Andrews, Maceo Woods, and many other gospel greats.

I can remember one night after one of our first recording sessions Lonnie was sitting at the dinner table discussing it with Mama. I was only half listening when he began to mention to Mama that the man at the recording studio thought that I (Neacie) had a spectacular voice. Neacie is the nickname my family gave me. I looked up just as Lonnie said my name. Mama looked towards me, then quickly glanced back at Lonnie, signaling him to be quiet. She didn't want me to hear that. I pretended I didn't know what was going on, turning my attention elsewhere.

Still that incident lingered in my mind. Why didn't Mama want Lonnie to let me know this? It was only a compliment. Perhaps she thought it would give me some ideas. Whatever the reason, I felt hurt. My God, can't I receive a compliment? Am I feeble or something? What was the problem? Why didn't she want me to hear that? Why did everything have to be received so negatively?

Of course, I kept those thoughts to myself; I knew better than to question Mama's reasons or decisions. Mama always knew what was best and her word was final, no matter how positive the idea may seem or regardless of it's potential. If Mama decided to keep it from flourishing, this was for my good. That was the mentality I was taught and raised by and to which my life conformed. What made it right, I do not know. Maybe because Mama said so. That was how she was raised, too.

Mama was from Memphis, Tennessee. She was the youngest in a family of eighteen children. Mama had a very strict and religious upbringing. She often told us about her childhood days and how she used to sing. Mama sang so well that her schoolteacher would enter her into various concerts and competitions. Mama was known throughout Tennessee for her skillful ability to sing classical and gospel music. She mentioned how she would stand boldly upon the stage in front of hundreds of people and belt out the popular tune "Is You Is Or Is You Ain't My Baby." That was one of the songs that gained Mama popularity throughout Tennessee. From that point on Mama's heart was set. She made up in her mind that when she grew up she was moving to Chicago and her next stop was Hollywood.

Mama's desire to be a star received no encouragement or support from her father, who was a Pentecostal minister, nor her mother, who didn't want her baby caught up into the cares of this life.

Mama never made it to Hollywood. By the time she turned seventeen she was on her way to Chicago where she met and married my Dad. That part of her dream came true. As for Hollywood, Mama would often say that God saved her and brought her over into Holy-wood. From that point on she sang nothing but the gospel.

As Mama's ministry progressed, following in her dad's footsteps and heeding to the call of Christ that was upon her life, she too, eventually became a Pentecostal preacher. Now that Mama's life was totally dedicated to the cause of Christ, she compelled her children to do the same.

Dad was also born in the South, in a small town named Flora, Mississippi; he laughed about saying it was so small it wasn't on the map. Dad was a handsome man, with medium brown complexion and standing at six feet tall. He was an only child who married mama, whom he met after moving to Chicago. He fathered ten children and became a construction worker.

Dad was basically a family man; the provider and breadwinner who would occasionally roll up his sleeves and make some of the best bread you could eat. I can remember the days he would come home, and after dinner he would go in the living room and lay down on the couch with his head in my lap, telling me to scratch his head. One day while looking down at this big bald spot lying in my lap, I finally gained the courage to tell him he didn't have no hair to scratch. He kindly told me to scratch around the sides where some hair still remained. I couldn't argue with that, so I proceeded in scratching his head until he would finally fall asleep. Then I would ease his head off my lap and quietly slip away.

Dad never had much to say about anything, no more than occasionally laughing and teasing with us. When it came to chastising us, Dad's size alone was intimidating. Every now and then he would fuss, but for the most part he left the disciplinary actions up to Mama.

Dad attended church faithfully, but even in that he was rather laid back. He was mostly there to assist Mama in the ministry God laid in her charge. Dad would fit in wherever he was needed, from taking the people to and from church, to driving the church's big diesel truck, which held all of the tent equipment used for Tent Revivals. Every year Dad would faithfully drive that truck to whatever state Mama was holding a revival.

I loved both of my parents. Dad was the man of the house, but Mama's strong will and authoritative character was our foundation. All of our knowledge and fear of God was instilled by Mama.

My siblings were my pride and joy. There was something in each one of them that I admired. Although we all had a close resemblance, each one of us had a unique characteristic.

Being raised in a religious home, we were taught the most important things in life were to love, fear, and serve God and to obey our parents. We were raised to be very high moral, clean, decent and respectful children. In spite of life's ups and downs, at that time I believed we were the American dream family. The most highly regarded and esteemed rule in our lives was for the children to remain virgins until marriage. I was most proud of this part of my life, until the day my virginity, along with my decision to marry, was taken away, beyond my control, and against my will.

CHAPTER 1

THE ARRANGEMENT

Between the ages of 12 and 13, I was very spiritually aware of God's calling in my life. I had a deep longing and sincerity to let His perfect will be done. There were times when, rather than jumping rope or playing games with my friends, I would choose to go with the saints (a holy people, professed followers of Christ) to convalescent homes, and various centers to visit the elderly and the shutins.

At that time I knew what I wanted to be in life, a traveling evangelist, ministering life and healing to God's people through preaching and singing the word of God. The Lord had given me a beautiful singing voice, and I asked God to anoint my voice so that people who hear me sing would be healed. This was my earnest heart's desire.

Since the age of seven I had become one of the church's main soloists, singing songs like *Precious Lord* and *Amazing Grace*. Mama often called on me to sing at church and outside engagements. I was proud to be my mother's daughter, and I tried hard to walk in her footsteps.

By the time I reached the age of 14, unknown to me, my life was about to have a serious change. I can remember the day Mama called me into her bedroom. She was sitting on the side of the bed as I walked in and sat beside her. She looked at me and said, "You're going to have to get married." I was shocked! I asked "Why?" In my mind I was wondering, what had I done? What's wrong with me? I'm a virgin, I don't fool around with boys, and I'm not one of those so-called "fast girls." So why do I have to get married?

While all those thoughts were going around in my mind, I managed to ask mama why and to whom? She told me I was to marry James, and the reason I had to marry him was because it was the will of God. I looked at her and said, "You prayed and

1

asked God for that didn't you?" She replied, "Yes." I responded back, "I don't want him, I don't know him, I don't like him, and he's too old for me."

Though I didn't know his exact age, I figured he was in his 20's and closer in age to my older sisters. I had seen him around the church, yet never paid him any attention. Again I repeated, " I can't marry him, I don't like him, why do I have to marry him?"

I liked one of the boys who were around my age named Steven. Steven and I would talk occasionally, but of course we weren't seriously involved. I knew I was too young for that. My goals were to finish school, and travel with the ministry. Perhaps by the time I reached my twenty-first birthday or older I would get married. I really liked Steven. His family and I were pretty close, too. Although we were pretty young, everybody knew we cared about each other, including mama. I would go over to Steven's house on Sunday evenings for dinner, and many other times when there was the opportunity to do so.

I can remember the first night Steven and his family came to our church. I had been playing with some of my little girlfriends sitting in the front row of church. I told them that the Lord was going to send me somebody, a young man of my desire who would grow up in the church and later become my husband.

That same night a lady walked into church during the service with six kids. There were three boys. Each one was nice looking, but of the three, I knew which one I felt was there especially for me. I turned grinning to my little friends. "I told you God was going to send somebody for me; that's him right there." I pointed towards Steven. Sure enough, word got back to me very soon that he liked me. I was so happy.

Remembering those things that happened about two years before my mother's announcement really affected me. Knowing that's where my heart was, I looked at mama and said, "I really like Steven, and if I can't marry him, I don't want anyone." That made her very angry. Mama looked at me and said sharply, "Steven doesn't want you; he wouldn't treat you right." Looking down I answered quietly; "I don't believe that."

Again, she insisted that I had to marry the man God had chosen for me. And if I didn't I would go to hell. I looked up scared and shocked. I repeated, "You mean, I'm going to go to hell if I don't marry James?" I sat there pondering. I knew I loved God. Why would He do this to me? Maybe there is something wrong with me; maybe I'm self-destructive and God is trying to save me from myself. I was hurt and confused.

Mama sat there. I can't remember everything else she said. All I can remember is her persistence. I was trying to sort out some questions, yet I knew she was waiting for me to say "Yes." With my head hung low in sorrow and fear, I figured she loved me and I knew I loved her and God. I wanted to please them both. I felt that I needed time. Against my will and out of fear and confusion, I said "O.K., but not now. I want to finish school." Content for the moment, Mama let me go. I left her room figuring I would make her happy, but on the inside I was so confused and miserable, and thought I had time.

Boy, was I wrong! A few days later, Mama sent James to talk to me. I was straightforward, as straight as a 14-year old girl can be, and to the point. I said, "Look! I don't like you, I don't know you, and I don't want to marry you. Since my mother said it's God's will, I'll marry you, but I want to finish school first."

James agreed and walked away. I had nothing else to say to him. He went back to Mama and told her what I had said. She told him I was only trying to play hard to get and that I really liked him. Later on she sent him to try and talk to me again. By this time I was irritated. Why couldn't they just leave me alone? I had agreed to what they wanted. All I wanted now was to finish school. We had plenty of time. After all, I was only in the eighth grade.

What I didn't realize was that Mama had no intentions of waiting. By the time my eighth grade graduation rolled around, Mama had invited James to my graduation. He was even dressed in the exact same colors I had on. I could be wrong, but I have reason to believe this was Mama's doing. I still have those pictures she suggested I take with him. I wanted to be with my friends, but instead I had to be with the man who was chosen for me. No one knew I was hurting on the inside, smiling on the outside. Only God knew my true thoughts.

During the time of my eighth grade graduation, I wore an engagement ring. I don't remember James giving it to me. All I can recall is that some days before graduation Mama decided that she, James, and I should look for a ring. I didn't want to go, but Mama seemed happy, so I went along.

I remember looking in the jewelry shop window. At that age, I was into birthstones, not diamonds. Since blue was my favorite color I picked a ring with sapphires circling a single diamond. I was ashamed to let my friends know about the imposed engagement. When they finally noticed the ring, I lied and told them it was my birthstone.

That evening I went downtown to dinner with my sister Janice, her friend Frank, and James. I sat through the entire evening wishing once again that I could be with my friends, wondering why couldn't I have gone out to dinner with Steven?

At that point, I went into what I called my imaginary world. In my imaginary world I could daydream I was surrounded by people I wanted to be with, and with Steven. Sitting there with those thoughts going through my mind, I could still relate to what was happening around me. There wasn't much conversation. I sat there trying to visualize how much fun I could have had, had I been with my friends. I quickly learned how to practice elusion. Whenever I was put into a situation I didn't want to be in or with someone I didn't want to be with, I would mentally escape to other places. In my imaginary world I was safe and happy. I could live my life as I desired with whom I pleased.

The dinner was OK, but I was glad when it was over and they took me home where my friends were eagerly waiting.

During that time Mama would write a major play every year, and I was always one of the main characters. I loved being in those plays. Mom was an excellent playwright. Her plays written then were comparable to the productions that I have seen

4

in the last several years. I noticed now when Mama would cast me; I was always playing opposite James. Because of this, I began to resent being in those plays. I was angry that James and I were always put together somehow in all of her plays. I didn't want someone they were forcing in my life. I changed my mind; I knew I couldn't marry James.

One evening when James came over to the house, I walked into my mother's bedroom and told her I didn't want to marry him, and I wanted to give him back his ring. She replied, " You don't want to marry him?" "No ma'am," I said. "Fine", she said. "Then take him back his ring." At that moment I was so relieved, I felt a weight lifting. I turned to walk down the hall, and into the living room to give James back his ring. Before I reached the threshold, I heard Mama yelling my name, calling for me to come to her. I turned and went back to see what she wanted. She said to me, "You better not do that!" Instantly I began to cry. I pleaded with her, *"Mama I can't do this, I don't like him, I don't want to marry him."* No matter how hard I cried, Mama wouldn't allow me to return the ring.

Many people from the church heard about the plan for our marriage. Tension was building. There were a few people who approved of the marriage; most were against it. Others were afraid to voice an opinion. I was trapped, trapped so badly I wanted to run away. I couldn't think of where to run. I had one sister who didn't live at home, and didn't go to church at that time, but I knew she greatly respected Mama and would probably send me back. I had to endure negative comments made by those who were strictly against this marriage saying things like, "He's robbing the cradle!" "She needs to go somewhere and sit her little fast self down!" This added to my hurt and shame.

My close friends felt sorry for me, for only with them did I share my true feelings. They knew I was being forced to marry this man. I was just not ready for marriage. I had my whole life ahead of me. With the growing tension, was the growing determination of my Mama to marry me off to James as soon as possible.

After a couple of months Mama called a meeting with me, my sister Janice, her friend Frank, James, and two other young couples in the church. As we came together, to our surprise Mama began to tell us this meeting was called to discuss marriage plans and arrangements. I sat up startled, "What? Not for me!" I was rebuked. So I sat there angry and shocked throughout this meeting that would change the course of my entire life. Finally Mama began to decide on a date. Janice begin to complain that she wasn't ready for marriage. Mama silently persuaded her, telling her if she didn't consent then I wouldn't. She felt if Janice agreed to marry then I would cooperate (which I found out later). First Mama decided we should get married in the month of June; I said July. She said December; I said January. Every month she said I would put it back further. Finally I was reproved into silence. Mama set the date, everyone else agreed (excluding me) and wedding plans began to roll into progress.

I almost had a way of escape. A few days later Mama took James and me to downtown Chicago for a blood test. The clerk said I was too young and had to be at least 16 years old even to be married with parental consent. I was so happy. I thought I would get away after all, but Mama was not to be defeated. She found out that the state of Alabama would marry you at fourteen with parental consent. So there I was about a week later, miserably on my way to Alabama with my mom, my dad, and James.

Some of you may wonder where my father fit into all of this? He was clearly against the marriage. He made this known to me one day when I walked up to him and asked for some change to buy myself some candy. Dad looked at me with disapproval and said, "What are you asking me for money for? Aren't you about to get married? Ask your husband." Those remarks hurt me so badly. All I could say was, "Daddy, that's not my fault." I walked away with heaviness and hurt in my heart.

My Dad never knew how much he hurt me. Although he never said anything else about this marriage, I knew he wasn't happy about the situation. Still he wouldn't dare speak against Mama's wishes.

To everyone that knew Mama, she was a woman of God whose authority was not to be questioned. Mama loved God and would do anything to please Him. I can remember how she would pray for hours in her closet days at a time. Many times Mama would go on shutins. This is a period of time when the minister would shut in away from the congregation to seek God through prayer and fasting. I trusted in Mama's walk with God. She was truly a God fearing, uncompromising, sanctified woman of God. She was God's servant and my role model. I wanted to know God like Mama did. This was the main reason I consented out of fear to this marriage.

After we got to Alabama, we changed clothes and went to the Justice of the Peace. All I can remember is Mama signing some forms. She seemed happy now and content. I can't remember anything more except for later on that night when we got back to the hotel. Mama looked at me smiling, asking me where I was going to sleep, now that I had a husband. I told her I would be sleeping right there with her and my dad, and so I did.

When we got back to Chicago, they proceeded to make plans for the wedding. My older brothers and sisters were now persuaded this was God's will. Those that weren't were made to keep silent. Still, they pitched in to help wherever it was needed. This was one of the largest weddings our church ever had. My three oldest sisters were already married to men of their choice, and their weddings were beautiful. But none of them was as extravagant as this one. Since four couples were getting married together, Janice, two other couples and myself, everybody that could wanted to be in this wedding. We had twenty four bridesmaids and ushers, twelve junior bridesmaids and junior ushers, twelve flower girls, four ring bearers, four maids of honor, and one matron of honor for me.

I remember the day the brides-to-be and I went with Mama to the bridal shop to choose our wedding gowns. I sat in the corner of one of the dressing rooms in a benumbed state, feeling as if I was in a dream, watching those around me prepare for something I was totally, helplessly against. I was so sad, but I knew I'd better not utter my thoughts. All I could think about was that my mom seemed happy, but I was miserable. Again I began to wonder, what had I done? What was wrong with me that God would do this to me? I neither liked nor knew this man. If God were going to give me a husband at least he could give me love for him. I felt nothing but a growing resentment toward this man they were forcing into my life. Yet, I hid it well.

So there I was, sitting in the bridal shop with conversations and commotion going on all around me, hoping this was just a dream. Unfortunately it wasn't. It was my turn to pick out my wedding gown. I really wasn't into this and didn't know what to look for. Finally, like any other little girl, I picked the dress with the lace top. Eventually each of the brides had chosen a dress of her choice. The more we got accomplished, the worst I felt.

A few weeks later we picked our cakes. Each bride chose her own. I picked a red and white cake, since the wedding was scheduled for Valentine's Day. As for invitations, I didn't send out any. I refused to invite any of my friends and relatives. I was ashamed of being married so young, and I was not happy.

There were enough people talking about me already. They wouldn't say anything around Mama, but they had a way of getting their points across to me. Who could I run to? Of course Mama would have only reproved me for listening and being foolish, and according to her they were just jealous.

Finally, the day arrived. It was on February 14, 1976, I remember it being a pretty cool day and rather cloudy.

When my family and I arrived at the church, people were scurrying about trying to get ready. I don't remember getting dressed or who helped me. I still couldn't believe this was happening. I wanted somebody, anybody to object. I stood in

Mama's office at the church waiting for everything to fall in place.

Again I went into my imaginary world where I was happy and marrying the man I loved. My imaginary world had become a crutch. I would escape there often, almost everyday now because it took me away from the sadness and confusion. I was learning how to cope with reality by being there and yet not being there, by creating an illusion.

I could hear the organ playing *"Here Comes The Bride"* as I stood behind the double doors, with my hand tucked under my dad's arm. As the doors opened, I looked through the veil that was pulled down over my face. Glancing across the congregation I was feeling no excitement, nor that happy nervousness that a bride is supposed to feel. I just tried to manage a straight face as my father and I took slow steps towards the altar, where the other brides and grooms were waiting.

I can vaguely remember the vows as the minister (Mama) addressed each couple separately to make the commitment and exchange the rings. Of course there was no passionate kiss for me, just a peck on the lips. Now it was all over. As the organist began to play the bridal party marched out first. They performed an arch for the couples as we marched through.

Following the cheerful sounds of congratulations and the throwing of rice, everybody went downstairs for the reception. I went looking for my friends. I wanted to play. Just as I was about to take off running one of my girlfriends stopped me dead in my tracks and reminded me, "You can't do that; you're married now." I stopped, turning to look at her, then down at the dress I had clutched in my hands preparing to run. The fact that I was dressed in a wedding gown had not crossed my mind; I was still a little girl.

Those words of my friend hit me like a blow. Although she didn't mean any harm I never forgot them. Perhaps those words were saying, or I interpreted them to be saying, "You're no longer a carefree little girl. You have to play the grown-up

9

game." I had some fast growing up to do. I hated that. That really dampened my already low spirit.

Yet I made it through the evening. I don't know how but I even managed to smile for the camera. I've always enjoyed having my pictures taken. Later on as I looked around the reception area before the crowd began to disperse, there was a deep sadness in my heart. I had none of my friends I grew up with or went to school with there, not even my best friend that lived across the street. Only my church friends were happily laughing and playing around, being the children they were. This was supposed to be the happiest moment of my life.

As the crowd was leaving I stood near the door watching my sister Janice get carried over the threshold. I don't know where the other two brides were, but I walked out of the church and climbed into the awaiting car with James. My new brother-in-law, Frank was driving. Janice sat in the front beside him. I didn't know where we were going and I didn't ask any questions. I went to sleep.

When I awakened I realized we were at a hotel. I had no idea where we were. This surely had not crossed my mind nor was I looking forward to this moment. I didn't want Janice to leave me, so we got adjoining rooms. After we checked in, Janice came into my room and talked to me for a few moments. After a while she got up and went to her own room where Frank was waiting.

Finally I went into the washroom to change clothes. I took off my wedding gown and put on a skirt and blouse I had brought with me. Keeping on my stockings and girdle. Then I took the beautiful white night gown my mother had bought for my wedding night. I put it on over everything else. I was tired and scared. Figuring I couldn't go to Janice's room, I slowly laid down on the very edge of the bed with my back to my new husband and fell asleep.

The next day, which was Sunday, we packed up our things, and went home (to my mother's house), and got ready for church. When we arrived at church everybody seemed to be looking at each bride for a certain sign. After realizing what was going on, I was glad I walked in still a virgin.

I can remember Mama often mentioning with pride, how I left a virgin and came back a virgin, and how for months, because my husband loved and respected, me he waited. I couldn't dare tell her I held out because I felt no emotion for this man. The hardest thing in the world is giving yourself to a man you don't love. I had always dreamed I would save myself for that special day and the special man I would marry. But there I was, the day had arrived much sooner than I expected, and it wasn't special.

Through all of this the one thing I had going for me was prayer. I prayed daily, asking God to please help me make this marriage work. Considering this was *God's* perfect will, I needed Him to give me love for this man He had chosen for me; *"after all God I did this for you"*.

Eventually I gave in. I started telling myself this was God's perfect will, and James and I were chosen to be an example to all the others. When all the other brides, who were married the same day as we were, became pregnant, I prayed and asked God to let me conceive a child also. I was earnestly trying to make things work. I felt that having a child would give me someone I could love.

During my pregnancy I was no longer with my peers. Instead I would keep company with the other young women who were pregnant. I wanted to appear happy and content, but inwardly I was struggling with an obligation to make things work. There was so much hurt from being forced into this predicament, yet still I pressed on. Eventually I learned how to talk to James at least casually, nothing really serious. The most he communicated to me was sexually. James was often in the mood for sex. No matter what time of the day or how I felt, I would cater to him. Other than that, we didn't really know each other. Everything else he wanted he would communicate to Mama. She would tell me what to do, when and how. Even to

11

the point of how to fix his plate, how to iron his clothes and how
to treat him.

CHAPTER 2

COMPLEXITIES OF GROWING UP

I was fifteen when I had my first child, a baby girl named Tefa. Mama was right there after her birth, helping me every step of the way. She kept Tefa while I finished school. She often took Tefa traveling with her from state to state. I loved Mama dearly; I was making her happy. This, and the fact that I was doing God's will, kept me going. Still that didn't change the fact that I yet had feelings for Steven. He and I couldn't talk anymore. It was forbidden that we have any form of communication. Every time Steven came around or just by chance was anywhere near me, Mama and James watched him, silently daring him to speak to me. He never would.

A few years later, Steven became involved with one of the young ladies, who was older than he. Everybody thought it was a disgrace. I felt he did that out of revenge. Feeling sorry for him, I told Mama I felt I was to blame for his situation. She rebuked me sharply.

Later on, when counseling was called for Steven and the young lady, I had to attend that meeting. As they announced their plans to marry, I sat there quietly with my heart aching. I knew I needed some serious deliverance. The worst is being married to one man, and still have feelings for another. Although it's sad, these things happen and life must go on.

Thank God I finished high school; now I was free to travel with the ministry. This was one of my greatest, life-long desires. I was licensed as an ordained minister at the age of fifteen. I ran my first week-long revival with another one of the youth ministers. As time went on, I became one of the keynote speakers during the bigger revivals, tent meetings and convocations. I always had a zeal for God. I loved Him and was definitely inspired by His wondrous works. I traveled annually with Mama and the Evangelistic team from one state to another ministering healing, saving, and delivering.

I loved singing and encouraging the people as I led the praise services, preparing them for the speaker. I was fascinated by the power of God! I sought Him daily that He would anoint my singing so people would receive deliverance just from hearing me sing. There were times God would do just that! All of this was so precious to me.

But there was still a problem at the beginning when we traveled. James was one of Mama's drivers, so naturally I always had to ride with them. I wasn't allowed to ride the other vehicles with the other young people. At times Mama would even place me in the front seat between her and James. I hated that! I wanted to be free, like the other children, to enjoy laughter and fun, not always being forced to be with James.

As time went on, James stopped traveling with us. That was a relief! I just didn't' appreciate someone being forced in my life. I felt smothered!

I had a hard time accepting James and his presence. I never missed him when he wasn't around. It caused me even more problems. When I traveled with the ministry and others would call back home to talk to their spouse or children, I never called James. I wouldn't even think to call him, not until Mama would call back home. Then she would send for me and ask me if I had called James. I would say, "No ma'am." She would either give me the eye or reprove me for being stupid. When I did call I never had much to say other than "Hello, How are you doing?" I couldn't pretend any emotions. I didn't mean any harm. The man didn't really cross my mind and I didn't miss him.

I was often reproved for how I treated James and was often told some other girl would have been glad to have him. I began to wonder, is this my fault? Why am I supposed to feel guilty? I felt nothing but sadness and constant pressure. This sort of admonishing had become a continuous cycle in my life. That's when I really began to detest my situation. As much as I loved Mama and no matter how hard I prayed there was always a problem because of my not loving James. Having been taught in church to go into the prayer closet, seek God earnestly and He would answer prayer, that's exactly what I did.

I begged God to give me love for James, to make me fall in love with him. At times I would shut myself up in my bedroom and weep bitterly. I wondered how long was I going to have to endure this. Many times I would sit and think of ways to run away, trying to figure out where to go. The only thing that kept me from making that move was the goodness of God. I knew I wanted to be saved and I knew if I left James I couldn't go back to Mama's church. That is where I wanted to be. I was convinced that had I left, Mama would have disowned me. Perhaps she would have sent someone looking for me, ridiculing me worse than before. Many times I wished I had taken that chance. Maybe in due time they would have forgiven me since I was so young. But like I said, I loved God, so I must endure.

It's difficult remembering some things; when I remember I relive all of the hurt, pain, confusion and frustration I felt back then. Every time I recall various moments of my situation, I get angry all over again. Sometimes I have to pause from writing to compose myself.

Things got worse as I became older, especially in the private part of our lives. In the first few years of my marriage, I catered to James because of a wife's responsibility to her husband. Now I had began to read Harlequin Romance books to either help me get in the mood or as an affectionate fulfillment. I began reading romance stories on a daily basis because the romantic situation just did not exist in my marriage. I became addicted to those books. They pacified the emptiness in my life. Many times if I didn't have a book I would make up my own stories in my mind. I daydreamed for hours about how my life could have been. The older I became, the more this was a problem.

By the time I reached eighteen, I'd become more distant. Many times when James wanted to touch me I would say "No." I got to the point where I couldn't stand for him to put his hands on me. I knew it was wrong according to the Scriptures since I

15

was his wife, but after five years I still felt no love for him. After all of the pleading and praying nothing happened. Of course, I wouldn't dare tell anyone. I had no one to express my problems to without being ridiculed. To make matters worse, when I would refuse James, he would go and tell my mother. Boy, did I get it! After she got on my case I would slowly walk back to my bedroom with mixed emotions of anger, frustration, and now a growing resentment. I would brace myself to fulfil my wifely duty. Forbidden to say what I thought or felt for fear of being preached to hell and back, I'd lie there with my eyes shut tight, as James did what he wanted and finish. Only God knew what I suffered mentally.

Year after year, I was told, by Mama "James is a jewel; you don't know how to treat him; you're just like your father." I was even told that maybe if I had gotten someone that would kick my tail, I would have been happy. To myself, I said maybe I would have. Angry thoughts rolled through my mind, yet I held my peace.

I've learned over the years that there isn't much difference between mental abuse and physical abuse. One harms your mind and the other harms your body, but they both break your heart and wound your spirit, which can also cause mental stress or depression.

By now I was so reclusive, if James approached me in my sleep, I would sleep through the whole sexual experience, never waking up during the entire procedure. That was how at 18 years old I conceived my second child, my son Lil James. God is my witness. When I missed my period the following month I thought maybe I'd miscounted. By the third month I was trying to figure out when did this happened? When I mentioned it to James he told me he knew exactly when and that I had slept through the whole encounter.

Now, I realize some may find that hard to believe, but you have to consider that in my time many men, especially men in church, did not try to please their wives. They just got on top, took care of their business, and by the time their wives were in the mood they were finished. Approximately two minutes. Some men did it out of ignorance, others out of no consideration. After he finishes, he turns right over and goes to sleep. And they wonder why their wives don't want to be bothered. It's hard to tell a man he left you hanging; you figure he should know. Being brought up as a virgin and made to marry so young, I went through that for years. Many times I slept through the whole ordeal.

After all those years I still didn't know James well enough or feel comfortable enough to say what I needed or wanted sexually. As stated before, he mostly communicated with me through Mama, especially when he was upset with me about something. James would go directly to Mama, who would of course straighten me out.

At one point in my marriage I had so many marriage counseling sessions. They were at least once or twice every week. I was always the guilty, ungrateful wife who didn't realize she had a jewel. James would sit through those meetings, never saying a word, except for the few complaints he had. Most times I was counseled without James being present; there was no need to counsel him; James was a jewel.

I would sit through those meetings hardly uttering a word. Many times my sisters would be there. They would state time and time again how I didn't realize what I had and how they would trade places with me. Had I been able to speak my mind I would have surely offered them the trade.

During those meetings not one time did anybody ask me why I was not receptive to him. Not once did one of my five sisters ever take me to the side and ask what was the problem. Nobody knew my pain. I don't think the thought that I was hurting ever crossed their minds. I was supposed to take what was given to me and be happy, be glad that somebody loved me. Which is crazy I'm a naturally nice looking young woman. I don't think I would've had a problem had it been someone I loved. Not discrediting James; he's a handsome man, but that didn't make me love him.

17

Perhaps if my family had used a different approach, I may have learned to love James in due time. I didn't say "fall in love." No one can make you fall in love. That's something that just happens on its own free will, sparked by attractions and emotions. When it comes to falling in love or being in love, the heart has a mind of it's own.

My family's constant badgering only caused a resentment to build up in me. Every time I looked at James I would think to myself, "If it weren't for you things would be better between my family and me." I wished a million times I had married someone they didn't care so much about. It was hard always being compared to a "jewel."

I grew up with a complex, always feeling like my sisters were better than I. They didn't seem to have any problems. They loved their husbands and enjoyed their marriages. Yes something was definitely wrong with me. I found myself often looking at James wondering, "Why?" Why can't I love him? He is nice looking, well built, a good father to our children and he's a good person. God! Something is really wrong with me. Why can't I feel something for this man?" I was often repenting to God for my negative feelings, begging Him to change them.

I wanted to make my family happy. I wanted to see what they saw in James. Not that I couldn't see it; I just wasn't attracted to him. I longed for happiness. Since no one ever asked, I never expressed why I felt the way I did. I realize now more than ever they were on the outside looking in.

My sisters didn't know what it was like to be in my shoes. They never had to walk in them. They were not given to someone they didn't like or really know at the tender age of 14. I was engaged in grammar school and had a husband before I attended high school. I was so ashamed. I resent that to this very day. They never had to experience many nights pretending to be asleep, hoping he wouldn't touch you. Holding your legs together so tight, many times wrestling when he becomes persistent. There's not much difference in the numbness a woman feels when she is being raped than when she's giving it up unwillingly. They both leave you with humiliation and a bitter resentment.

My dear sisters never had to live that experience. Yet they could sit back and boldly state their opinions. Still, I never uttered a word. Year after year I let all of this build up. Many times I wished James would walk away and leave me. That way I wouldn't be looked upon as the bad guy.

I can remember one time during one of my counseling sessions, Mama stated how sad I would be if James walked off and left me. The idea was such a pleasant one. I burst out laughing. I just couldn't picture that making me unhappy. Of course Mama didn't think that was funny.

One day I was even labeled as being like a slut and was told I had a "whore's forehead." In other words, since I didn't love James, then I just wanted to be laid up with other men. I had never slept with another man in my entire life. In spite of all the unhappy circumstances and conditions, I remained faithful. Knowing fornication and adultery were definitely wrong, I wasn't about to go to hell for that. Furthermore, the little I learned about sex in my relationship with James, wasn't worth losing my soul.

When I was growing up, two situations arose. One of the young men in the church became attracted to me. It was not a deliberate situation. At this time I had begun to spend more time around the youth, working with the choir and the music ministry. The young people would often come over to our house and sit around eating, laughing and talking. I enjoyed working with the youth. They had become like my very own children. More than a ministry, they were my family. I loved them and many of the young people admired me.

Each time one of the young men became attracted to me and I to them, I went to the pastor, who was my mother, and confessed my faults. I didn't want to get my soul in trouble. I was sincere with God. I knew I had a calling on my life and it must be fulfilled. I couldn't afford to be a failure; I believed that God would literally kill me.

Therefore, before anything could happen, I confessed my faults in front of the entire church and repented. But before I was allowed to confess and repent to the church, we were taken into a council meeting. We were both reprimanded for even entertaining the very thought of lust. Again I was reminded of the jewel God gave me.

The second time this type of situation occurred, I went and confessed my faults. This time after the meeting not only did I confess and repent to the church, but I crawled down the aisle and knelt at James's feet, repenting to him.

After that last incident I fought twice as hard to give my life totally to God. I needed some fulfillment. I believed that if I gave myself totally to God, I would be able to deal with everything else. I became even more dedicated to the ministry. God began to bless the works of my hands. In return, I grew to have a closer walk with Him. At times I would sit in the midst of the service while the pastor was up ministering, and I would silently ask God to speak to me through prophecy. Before that service ended prophecy (inspired predictions-spoken through the mouth of a prophet or minister), would come through unto me. My love and dedication to God was so intense, I just wanted to please and serve Him more. This was my strength.

My ministry had begun to elevate. When Mama would go on a shut-in, (when a minister sacrifices through fasting and praying for a certain length of time, usually shut away from the people to go before God), myself, along with a few other ministers, were left in charge of the church. I can remember one time when she was shut in for seven days. I was one of the ones left in charge to run a revival those days. I felt grateful that out of all of my sisters, being the second youngest, that God chose me. That was one of the greatest revivals I'd ever run. My mom was pleased when she came out of the shut-in. I was so happy and grateful to God.

The Lord was beginning to really use me. I prayed daily that He would make me one to forever stand by the side of His servant, my mother.

CHAPTER 3

TRIALS, TRUTHS, AND CHALLENGES

In 1982, my eldest brother Lonnie, who was the assistant pastor of the church, was killed. He was shot down by a cop in a racially motivated incident. That was another one of the most devastating moments of my life. I was pregnant during the time. Two months after that incident I had my third child, Denise.

Through those times Mama fought to be strong for the rest of us, but I knew Lonnie's death hurt her more than life itself. Yet she would never let us see her cry.

Lonnie and Mama had a great oneness in the ministry. After his death, I vowed to stand by the side of my mother in the ministry like never before. I held nothing back from her, good or bad. I wanted the Lord to knit us together with a oneness like she had with Lonnie. I wanted to be there for her, to fill that empty ache his death had left behind.

I became so like Lonnie in my ministry, Mama would often say she could see his face in mine. Those that knew him began to often speak of the resemblance between Lonnie and me. I was so happy. Finally I would amount to something. Now I could really please God and prove I could stand by the side of His servant. Life was beginning to look up for me. My family was proud of me at last.

I was dedicated to that ministry; traveling, singing, preaching, fasting, praying, standing firm in defense of the gospel, working with the youth, setting up street services and park services to keep them spiritually motivated. I organized various programs to inspire them educationally as well as spiritually. The youth services were some of the most invigorating services we had in the church. Everyone would be excited to attend service on the youth night. They would come out with great expectations that God would surely bless the service, and He did! We were sincere and our services were good.

As the years went on, God had begun to really bless me. Being so busy in the ministry, I could now cope better with my marriage. I was determined to make it work, to make myself love James. I can remember so clearly the time I buckled down and said I would make myself think of him during the course of the day. I would go out and buy him things for various occasions. I learned how to communicate with James more.

One day, after everyone left the house except James and me, I called him into the kitchen and told him we needed to talk. I addressed the problems we were having, with the main one being we didn't communicate. I told James he could no longer run to Mama and my family every time he had a problem with me. If he wanted to be treated like a man, then he had to stand on his feet and act like one. This was the only way James could earn my love and respect. I told him I wasn't a little girl anymore. Neither did he have to run to Mama and tell as if I was his little sister. James agreed to try. It was hard for him at first. My family was definitely a crutch for him.

One day James came downstairs into the kitchen where Mama, two of my sisters, and I were talking as we prepared dinner. I don't remember the exact conversation, but it was leading towards me, at that moment James got ready to say something to Mama about me. I caught his eye with a knowing expression. He kind of grinned, unsure of what to do. I stated, "I'm not playing with you." The others did not catch on, but James knew what I meant.

It happened a few more times, and finally I managed to straighten him out. I was tired of my family running my marriage. We were close, but I knew at some point I had to draw the line. Furthermore, our marriage was the only marriage everyone knew everything about. That was the thing I envied most about my sisters' marriages. In comparison to mine, they were so obviously different. My marriage was always used as an example one way or the other.

My sisters' children had begun to make jokes about my having James sleep on the floor. The worst part was when the children grew older and began to ask why I got married so young. They weren't quite sure how young. I never talked to them about it, but either their parents or someone else did. My marriage had always been difficult to talk about.

I was always ashamed to tell anyone how old I was when I got married. If they would try to guess, I would avoid answering and finally change the subject. That is something to this very day I find hard to talk about. Not just because I was ashamed, but the older I got the harder it was to tell them it was God's will. Especially in this day and time, many people have a hard time accepting that.

Actually I had begun to wonder myself, which reminds me of a specific incident that happened a few years ago in 1992. I was carrying my last child, D'Angelo, when I got my real answer.

THE TRUTH

I will never forget that day as long as I live. Mama and my sister, Janice, were in the kitchen cooking. I was sitting there in a chair talking to my mom as she walked back and forth preparing dinner. I don't remember the entire conversation. It was pretty serious. For the first time in sixteen years, it gave me the opportunity to ask Mama why she married me off so young. I'll never forget that moment. She looked at me after pausing for a moment and said, **"To keep down confusion in the church."** She said there were quite a few girls in the church that were after James. Some of the mothers were trying to get him for their daughters. So to keep down the confusion, she planned my marriage to James.

I went through a total state of shock, disbelief, anger and God knows what else in a matter of minutes. I was speechless and my thoughts were heavy. Even though I didn't utter a sound, in my mind I said, "You mean to tell me I went through all of this because of that? I went through all of that pain and confusion for nothing?" Not only was I angry, but I was hurt and didn't quite know how to feel. If I ever needed God's help I surely needed it then. Lord, what had they done to me?

Perhaps you're wondering what was so special about James. He was a virgin. That alone made my Mama feel he was special and deserved the best, another virgin. Since some of the other girls in the church had a street life before God saved them, they were not good enough.

Just to think, all that time I thought I was doing God a service. I thought of the many trials and tribulations I encountered because I wasn't happy. Some of those same girls that wanted James, resented me and wanted to harm my children. One of them had even confronted me saying, she knew I didn't want James, and that he should have been given to her. The list goes on and on. *And I went through all of that for what?*

Although I had asked that question a million times in my mind, perhaps I would have been better off not knowing. The things I held in for years began to spill out little by little, my thoughts, my anger, my resentment, and my regrets. None of this was towards my Mama. No matter what she did I loved her more than anything in the world. But little by little, whenever the occasion arose, I let James and others know how I felt.

I stopped pretending, stopped trying to force myself to feel something that just wasn't there. I couldn't hurt James by telling him I never loved him. I did sit and talk to him a few times about how I resented the way they handled my life. I told James I didn't believe God had anything to do with his being chosen for me. God may have approved it because His servant, Mama, asked Him. I didn't think it really mattered who I married as long as I loved him and he was saved and God fearing.

I wasn't trying to hurt James. I had no one else to turn to and release the things I felt. All those things, I had held in for years. Even those things I thought were a sin to share with someone. All those years I felt in the depths of my heart and soul that something was wrong. To find out I was right was heartbreaking. I had spent years trying to condition myself for something that should have never been. God, you've got to help me now!

My wounds began to reopen. Over a period of time everything on the inside of me begin to unravel. I started releasing the pain that seemed to never go away. After finding out the truth, I no longer pretended I was happy. Still I tried to stay focused on my ministry; regardless of the continuous confusion in my life, I was always out somewhere singing or preaching.

People would often ask if I was married or if I had any children. I would politely answer yes, mentioning that I had four children, then kindly change the subject. But you know how some people are. They want to know how many, their age, and gender.

Because my children are as big as I am, people often think my oldest daughter is my sister. Upon seeing my children, people automatically want to know how old I am or how old I was when I got married. Sometimes I would explain that my marriage was arranged, or I would laugh and say "I was a Chinese bride." Which only made them curious as to what a Chinese bride is. I would then explain that over in China and other foreign countries, they have arranged marriages, where young girls are betrothed to men their parents have chosen for them.

This would bring about expressions of total shock or exclamations of disbelief that something of this sort was being practice in the twentieth century. This led to other questions about how I felt and how was I dealing with it. My answer was, "By the grace of God," and then ending the conversation.

THE CHALLENGE

The thing I feared the most has happened to me...

I figured the only way to keep my life under control was to stay involved in my ministry. This was my refuge. I began getting the youth choir involved with the traveling ministry along with accepting singing engagements in the inner city. We were definitely on the move for Christ. I loved God's people and strove to reach out to everyone from every walk of life. I met hundreds and thousands of people from various ministries. The ministry God had laid in my trust inspired them.

One day while at a television taping with my choir I met a young man name Robert. He was one of the musicians for one of the other groups that were present. During the taping Robert was sitting across the isle from me. I wasn't paying any attention to him until my friend Wanda, who was sitting next to me, touched me saying; "Look Sister Neacie, that guy over there is laughing at you." As I glanced towards him, Robert was laughing so hard I almost got offended. When I took a closer look at him I had to smile. This guy just seemed to enjoy laughter. Yet I was still curious as to what and why was he laughing. He didn't know me except through the brief introductions made prior to the show.

After the taping I kindly walked over to Robert and asked if he was laughing at me. "No," he said. He began to laugh again. "I was laughing at the guy who was up there trying to sing." That led us into a short conversation during which I invited him and his group to my church's upcoming program. Before leaving we exchanged numbers.

A few days later Robert called me. He was so easy to talk to. He had one of the deepest sensual voices I ever heard. I tell you the brother was another "Barry White". No, don't get me wrong; he wasn't flirting. The brother just had a gifted set of pipes. The conversation was casual and polite.

During our first conversation I can remember Robert asking me if I was married. I answered "Yes" and then asked if that was a problem. Did that mean he didn't want to be my friend? He seemed to hesitate a moment, so I hung the phone up on him. I was shocked when I realized what I'd done. I wondered to myself, "why did I do that?" I had never hung the phone up on anyone before. I just knew he wasn't going to call me back. To my surprise, he did. I apologized immediately. Overwhelmed with shame and embarrassment, I began to explain how I had never hung up on anyone before. I was earnestly sorry. In spite of that little incident we became friends, which was no great challenge for me. I had other friends in the ministry and I was highly respected by them. I was always careful and straightforward. I figured Robert was just another brother in the Lord. As time went on Robert and I grew closer. Robert was always there for me. Many times when I had engagements to sing or preach, Robert would be there. He became my best friend. This was the first time a man had ever befriended me in such a way. Just talking to him made me happy. I had found someone with whom I could share my inner most feelings. Eventually I gave him my life story. I was usually apprehensive to talk about it. As I revealed my hurts and silent frustrations, Robert would listen attentively. He never judged or criticized me. He understood me. I could tell my situation without feeling guilty. In turn, he began to share with me the things he was going through. For the third time, he was separated from a marriage he had continuously tried to save. This time he and his wife were heading for divorce. I could hear the pain in Robert's voice as he shared his problem. His life was falling apart. In spite of circumstances he was determined to develop his ministry with God. This is what I admired about him the most. He was strong in the Faith. We shared a deep spirituality. I grew to really appreciate Robert's friendship.

Late one evening Robert called me revealing his true feelings. He really cared about me. He didn't want to cause any problems in my life so he felt we should end our friendship, concluding that he didn't think he should call me anymore. As polite as possible I told him he would get over it. I didn't think it was so serious that he had to stop calling me. Furthermore, I didn't want to lose my friend.

Truth is, I shared the same struggle. For the first time in my life I was challenged with emotions I'd never felt before. By golly this thing was real! I honestly loved him. Talking about a trial of my faith! Whew! I was like the songwriter, "What Is This?" I'll tell you one thing. It ain't no joke!

I couldn't tell Robert in the beginning. I had to be strong for both of us. We were trying so hard to keep things in the right perspective. It wasn't easy. The more I heard from him, the more I needed to hear from him. I prayed daily for God's help. I knew Robert was fighting too. Sometimes he wouldn't call me for about three days. But we could never seem to get pass that length of time without communicating. We were fighting a losing battle.

Still I kept praying and fasting about this situation. What was so strange, the more I prayed the stronger my feelings grew towards Robert. God, why? Why would you torture me like this? Why would you let me meet this man knowing I would love him and can't have him? I prayed to God *daily*. I was experiencing emotions, on a level I had never known, for the first time in my life. I was actually in love.

This was the thing I feared. I had never cared for anyone else like I cared for Robert. I knew it was wrong, but if I can borrow a phrase from Stevie Wonder, "how could something so wrong feel so right?" My heart needed to know.

Eventually Robert and I sat down and had a serious talk. I was torn between two thoughts, leaving with the man I loved or remaining in a situation I dreaded and resented. Lord God, what do I do? I really wanted to do the right thing. Do I follow my mind or my heart? Would God forgive me? Lord, what is really going on? First I find out that I was really misguided into this marriage. Then you send along the man of my dreams. What am I supposed to do? I was scared, hurting and confused. I was in a no-win situation.

I begged God to strengthen and help me through this struggle. Why me? Why now? Lord, what do I do? Who do I turn to? I knew if I told my family, I'd be criticized. I would be called dumb and stupid and told I'm just like my father all over again. It would reopen the wound, the "Pandora's Box" that held all the negative labels I'd managed to overcome.

28

Oh boy, I knew I had it coming. I would surely be scandalized. So I said nothing. For a long time I had to deal with my inner turmoil. Had I been available, I would have married Robert.

Life was a constant trial. Yes, I knew right from wrong. I'd never felt this way before. What really made it hard was the fact that I enjoyed the feeling of loving and being loved by someone of my own choice. A free flow of love without dictation is what I desired. Yes, it was wrong and forbidden, but to anyone that dares to tell the truth, the heart feels good when it is loved. Just to hear Robert's voice over the phone or to see him walking down the street, my heart would swell with emotions. I felt like a nervous teenager. Sometimes the brother made me feel speechless! Can I be real?

This is the thing I had been denied. My heart longed for love. That's what made it so painful. Now that I'd found love or it found me I was forbidden to entertain it. Talking about a frustrating situation; this was another great challenge in my life. Sure I was saved, had a thriving ministry under a strict doctrine. I wore no make-up, jewelry, or pants, I did no dancing, partying, or even visiting the movies. This was my sacrifice. I would do anything for the God of my salvation. But like the Apostle Paul, I had a thorn in my flesh. Many times I sought God for deliverance. Yet time and time again, in spite of myself, I still had a desire for true love.

Secretly I envied my sisters. For each of them had husbands of their own choice and experienced what I thought was "true love". Sometimes I would sit and watch as they laughed and played with their husbands. That must have been a beautiful feeling. It wasn't a forced laughter or a forced relationship. Lord, how I longed. Again I wondered why I couldn't have had a normal life? Time and time again I'd go and close up in my bedroom, weeping silently.

I began trying to convince myself that God didn't want me involved in a marriage based on love. Therefore I would give all of my love and attention to Him. I didn't have any problems with that. Jesus was definitely the center of my joy. Even from a child as far back as I can remember, I loved God and wanted to please Him no matter what. So Lord, why so much pain?

As time went on I realized I needed help to get out of this situation. I knew I was fighting a losing battle. I was so emotionally involved with Robert. I didn't have the strength to let him go. We were not sexually involved with one another in spite of our strong attraction. I was faced with the dilemma of being married to a man I never loved and in love with a man I couldn't have. God, please forgive me even now.

Wanting to do the right thing, one day I called Robert, we agreed to stop communicating. I knew it would be hard. So I pleaded with Robert not to call me back if I paged him. That was another hard thing to do. For I honestly loved him and never wanted to hurt him. It hurt me so bad having to let him go. Still I knew I couldn't do this alone. I figured Robert was stronger than I.

After hanging up the telephone I cried. My heart ached. The pain was so overwhelming I slid off the side of the bed to the floor. Tears streamed down my face, as my hand clutched my chest. I could hardly breathe. I had never experienced anything like this before in my entire life. After enduring this torture for a few moments I reached over and picked up the phone dialing Robert once again. At first, he didn't respond. I must have paged him about six or seven times before he finally called me back. I knew he was trying to grant my previous wish, but I couldn't take the pain. When Robert finally called, I broke down telling him I couldn't do it. I didn't want him to leave me. I was frightened by the intensity of the pain. Robert was hurting too. Yet realizing this was something that must be done, a few days later we gave it another try.

This time I fought to endure the overwhelming pain I knew was coming. At the same time I hated myself for falling in love. For weeks and months afterwards I cried in my sleep. Robert would be in my dreams; I could hear his voice so clear. It was so real I would wake up trembling and crying. It felt like the pain would last forever. Night and day I begged God to make the pain go away. Pleading and asking, dear God, why did you let this man into my life? You knew I would love him and that I could not have him.

To hear songs, that Robert used to sing, would cause me to break down in tears. Many times I was driving alone in my car crying so hard. I had to pull over to the side of the road to compose myself. Why didn't somebody tell me love could hurt so terribly? I once heard a saying that it was better to have loved and lost than to have never loved. I beg to differ; it would have been better if I had never loved. As the saying goes if it weren't for bad luck, I wouldn't have luck at all. There were days I would drive pass Robert's job longing to go in and talk to him, just to see his face one more time. Each time I lost the courage and I figured he didn't want to see me anymore. I neither saw nor heard from him again over the years. Yet year after year my heart ached for the only love it had ever known. Robert was gone.

A CRY FOR HELP

Finally I decided to go to the only person I knew could help me, my mother. Early one Sunday morning, I was so troubled and restless, I got up and went downstairs to Mama's house. We lived in this large beautiful two flat building in the south suburbs. I lived in the upstairs apartment. Mama and my sister Sharlett lived down stairs.

Mama was in her front living room, kneeling down praying as usual. I interrupted her quietly before I lost my courage, saying, "Mama I need to talk to you; I need help." She sat up and looked at me, listening as I began to tell her the situation between Robert and me. She waited patiently until I finished. She then said, "You really care about him?", I answered, "Yes ma'am." She asked, "Do you think he cares that much about you? I answered again, "Yes ma'am." She replied, "You're a fool!"

Truth is, I believe Mama knew I loved Robert. Before we decided to part, he used to come visit us at the church and the house. This lasted until she expressed he wasn't welcome anymore. To hear me say, I loved him was more than she could bear. To her I was not in love, I was in a lust rut, plotting to hurt her. I never meant to hurt her.

I knew I had it coming. Don't get me wrong. I deserved the rebuke, which I won't repeat, except for the very statement that hurt me to my soul. She said, "If you think you're hurting me by doing this, you got another thought coming!"

I sat there speechless. Mama went on saying I probably made it up just to worry her. It didn't phase her in the least. By then I found my tongue. I pleaded, "I came to you for help, I'm not trying to hurt you". Lord this was worse than I thought. Being rebuked was one thing, but being thought of as trying to hurt or betray the only mother I had and loved more than my very own life, was more than I could bear. Oh God, what had I done?

By the time Mama finished talking to me I was hurt and sick. Everything was hurting, my heart and my head. My body felt like lead. There was so much pressure on my mind. I was so bound I couldn't lift my head up. After pleading for forgiveness and asking for help, I slowly dragged back upstairs to my apartment, into my bedroom. With the little strength I had left, I laid curled upon my side. As I lied on the side of the bed, tears streamed down my face while praying silently. To this very day that's one confession I wish to God I had never made. Slowly but surely the relationship I fought to build for years with Mama began to disintegrate. I was reproved and rebuked about that situation over and over. Many nights in church I was reproved again and again. Many times at home I was reminded of how I was a big fool.

Then it began to get worse. I was not allowed to preach anymore. My portions in the church were being limited. Yet I struggled to stay a part of that ministry. I tried holding on to the youth services, but they were not the same. I couldn't shake the guilt. No matter what I tried, repenting, begging and apologizing constantly, I couldn't regain that closeness mom and I once had. As long as mom hadn't forgiven me I felt God hadn't forgiven me.

One year went by. On my own, I began to go on long fasts. Usually the church would fast together as a whole. Everything I did or tried was rejected. Still I struggled to hold on to the youth prayer on Mondays along with other special services that kept the youth involved. From parades, memorial services, and holiday programs, I kept trying. I had to.

Going into the second year, I felt God still hadn't forgiven me because Mama was still rejecting me. For I had sinned by falling in love with another man. Of course according to the church, it wasn't love. It was lust. I was being punished. Things continued to get worse. The distance between Mama and me was getting worse. After a long period of time, I was allowed to preach twice. Following each sermon I was counseled and rebuked. I realized then, no matter what I did I would never be forgiven.

Going into the third year, I was still allowed to go on the evangelistic trips with the traveling ministry; it was not the same. I was constantly reproved for one thing or another, so I tried staying in my hotel room to avoid being a problem. There was just no way of escape. God, I was miserable. I vowed to never go on another trip with the ministry. I could stay home and be a burden.

At this point my hope was diminishing, my spirit was dying, my hurt was unbearable. I was useless. After three years there was still no forgiveness. I had read many scriptures on forgiveness, but according to Mama's behavior, none seem to fit my case. Ephesians 4:32: "And be ye kind one to another, tenderhearted, forgiving one another, even as God for Christ's sake hath forgiven you." Although Mama tried, I knew she could never forgive me for my betrayal of the trust she had in me. I had let her down, wounding her beyond repair. At times I could see her trying to reach out to me but it was never the same.

As the realization of this sunk in, little by little I let go of everything that I was struggling to hold on to. I stopped coordinating special services. No longer was I a part of any revivals or convocations. I would only participate in the special services during which, I would only do presentations. Even in that I would pray to God for acceptance. I had become so fearful of rejection. Eventually I got to the point of just attending church. Every time I went to church I sat in the front row, finally moving to a corner. I was constantly reproved openly during the sermon. I would sit there enduring the pain. Oh God, how my heart ached. So many nights I sat in that church with tears streaming down my face, silently asking God, how long? Will you ever, ever forgive me? Please! I could feel the slight stares of those sitting around me and in back of me. Some had eyes filled with pity. Others shared my pain but were too afraid to even speak words of encouragement, for fear of becoming the next victim. It was understood that you did not communicate with anyone that was considered an outcast.

Every now and then when there weren't too many people around, someone would walk up to me and say; "I have to give it to you; you are strong. I don't see how you can take it". Others would say; "Hang in there', God is going to fix it. You're tough; you can make it".

To be truthful, my family and church were killing my very spirit, my will to live. The only thing I had left at this point was working with the youth choir in services, which I no longer had the strength to direct. There were still counsel meetings where I was constantly reminded of my failures. At this point my only friends were confusion, pain, and a false hope.

In the midst of all this came the fateful day I was called into a meeting to be told I would be relieved of my title as the Jr. Pastor until I got myself together. I really had nothing left; all I had was a title and now that was taken. I wasn't one that cared for titles anyway. I just loved the job of working in the ministry. Slowly but surely I went down to nothing, becoming totally non-functional.

The rebukes and the counseling meetings were increasing. They would always consist of Mama, two of my other sisters, (Janice and Fran) and me. No matter what the meetings were supposed to have generated from, before it was over, these famous lines were repeated. *You lost your portions for nothing. Your husband is a jewel. You never appreciated him. Anybody else was always better. And you're just like your father.* I sat through those meetings at first, trying to plead for forgiveness, apologizing over and over, constantly trying to get an understanding.

After a while I no longer had the strength to plead my case. I would just sit and listen until it was over, then go away, headed straight for a place to hide and weep. No matter how many times I went to the altar or kneeled at Mama's feet, I was never accepted. Now I had closed up, away from the entire world. At home I would be closed up in my bedroom, and at the church I would sit off in a corner. No one reached out to me.

One particular day, I was called into another counsel meeting. This time when those famous lines were repeated about my husband being a jewel, I raised my head from the palm of my hands, because I knew I had it coming. At that time, my pain had become more unbearable than ever. My heart ached. It was so heavy. I was so pressured and so full of pain.

Slowly I lifted my head; speaking out for once in my life I said, "If he was such a jewel, then why did you give him to me? For years, all I've heard was he's a jewel and I'm just like my father. Why did you give him to me? I didn't want him." After 17 years, I felt relieved speaking the truth I dared not to speak years ago. Though it was only for a brief moment. Janice and Fran sat there quietly not daring to say a word, no doubt thinking I had finally snapped or had lost my mind. After a moment, Mama quietly asked, "You don't want him?" "No ma'am," I said. Then I looked into her face trying to read her expression. Thinking I had hurt her, I tried to retract that statement, the truth that I had held in for so long. I tried to fix it up by saying, "Well I want him now." She stopped me by holding up her hand. "No

35

you don't," she said. Then she just sat there looking at me, saying nothing. For a moment, everything seemed quiet.

I couldn't say another word. I felt so tired and weary. My emotions were mixed with relief by finally telling what was in my heart, and sadness of knowing the truth seemed to hurt Mama. Why? Why should I feel bad for telling the truth? I needed to tell the truth. Had I known what it would cost me, I would have kept on living a lie.

I'll never forget that day as long as I should live. The truth seems to have cost me the mending of the most important relationship in my life, my mother and me. Mama didn't realize I could never love James because he seemed to have taken her love for me. I wanted her to love me for whom I was, not for who I married. Why did she seem shocked when I told her I didn't want him? Prior to being forced into this marriage, I cried and begged her not to make me marry him. Mama, why?

In spite of the fact that mom never told me that she wouldn't forgive me, I knew I'd destroyed her confidence in me. After that meeting, she didn't bother to talk to me alone anymore. Every time Mama wanted to talk to me she would send for my two sisters, Janice and Fran. I had to endure the most humiliating counsels in my life, always in front of an audience. Constantly in the presence of those two was I reprimanded and scorned.

I had already grown up, thinking that all my sisters were better than I. Now this feeling deepened. Sometimes I wished I could die or that I'd never been born. I was the only daughter mother had that caused her so many problems. My life was miserable. If only I could have been more like my sisters!

One Sunday morning as I was preparing to go to church, Mama called me downstairs, stating that she wanted to talk to me. I walked in and sat on the couch across from where she was seated. Before she began to talk or send for Janice and Fran, I asked, "Please, in all due respect, can I say something? I know you're my mother and you can do whatever you want, and I pray I'm saying this right. I just want to say, please don't call my sisters in here. You can talk to me alone. I'm your daughter too, just like they are. This one time please understand I already have a complex; please talk to me without them. "

Inwardly I was praying that I was saying this in an acceptable manner. Not meaning any disrespect, this was the one time I wanted to take my reproofs alone. Mama looked at me quietly for a moment. Then silently granting my request, she began to speak. The subject again was that I'd lost my portions with God. When Mama finished, I looked up carefully and said, "you have often told me I lost my portions. Could you please tell me how to get them back? What do I have to do? Please tell me something!" I was pleading for some sort of mercy, guidance, anything! Help! I knew I would do anything she said. All I wanted was to be accepted again, by her and by God.

Mama looked me in the eyes and said quietly, "Just pray." Slowly I exhaled after taking a deep breath. At this point I was getting frustrated. Nothing was working for me. I thought I was trying in every way possible. I mentioned this to her and again she looked at me and said, "Just pray." With my head hung down I sat there for a moment, then I arose quietly, so despondent, and walked away.

CHAPTER 4

THE WORST MOMENT OF MY LIFE

By now I only went places with the ministry if I was invited. Most of the time I stayed behind figuring what's the use? I had become a spiritual outcast. My strength was gone. That particular year, when the ministry had decided to take a trip I vowed within myself that I would not go. I knew my presence would only be a burden. I couldn't bare another trip like that.

Mama would always make a list of who would be going. I just knew my name wouldn't be on that list. I was prepared to stay behind. To me, I had no real part in the ministry any more. Why tag alone only to be a burden?

To my surprise, the day they were preparing to leave I had walked into my mother's kitchen to get a bite to eat. Mama was sitting at the kitchen table. She looked up at me as I moved around the kitchen and asked, "Are you going?" I was shocked! Mama seldom talked to me. Occasionally she would, but we no longer had that open communication we used to have. I answered, " I didn't think my name was on the list". She replied, "There is no list. I didn't make one."

I stood there with very mixed emotions. I was glad and shocked, although Mama had asked me, I was scared. I wanted to go because she had asked and she really seemed to want me to go, but inwardly I knew there would be problems. Finally my fear outweighed everything else. I dropped my head and said, "No ma'am." She looked at me and asked, "You're not going?" Again I said. "No ma'am." She said quietly, "All right."

It hurt me to tell her "no", but I couldn't face another trip as an outcast just tagging alone. I went outside as they were packing to leave. I had to take my oldest daughter to school so we said our good-byes to everyone and drove off.

Inwardly I was disturbed. I kept feeling like I needed to go on that trip, yet I was frightened, still I felt compelled. Midway to taking my daughter, Tefa, to school, I turned the car around and headed back towards the house. I had to catch up with my Mama and the saints. I went to the house first, but they weren't there, then I figured that they had to gas up first before leaving. I drove around the block to the nearest gas station. Thank God! They were still there.

Jumping out of the car I ran to the pay phone to call James to come pick up the car and take Tefa to school. Then I ran over to Mama's car, no luggage, no money, just me and D'Angelo, my baby boy. I climbed in the back seat between my sister Clara and a young lady who lived with us named Eloise. As I climbed in I said to Mama, " I'm going with you." She didn't look too pleased as she turned her head around. Looking at me she asked, "Why did you change your mind?" She didn't seem happy to have me along after all, but I went anyway.

Little did I know this would be the last trip I would ever take with my mother again. Now I can see that against all odds, God worked in my favor. He knew that if I had missed that trip I would have never forgiven myself. It was rough as I knew it would be, but considering it was the last one with Mama, it was worth it!

MY LAST DAYS WITH MY DEAR MOTHER

A while after we had come home from that last trip, Mama wasn't feeling too well. She had lost her appetite and had become weak. I figured she was going through a trial of some sort, and as usual God would eventually pull her through as he had done many times before. During this time, although things were still strained between us, I longed daily just to sit at her feet as she lied on the couch. I wanted so badly to tell her how much I loved her.

Everyday when I came in from school I would check in on her to see how she was doing. Many times she would look at me and nod. She would say, "I'm fine." Every morning before I went to school I would kneel beside my bed and pray for

Mama's deliverance. I didn't know what was really wrong because she never complained much about anything. Yet many mornings I knelt and wept before God for her complete deliverance.

Although I felt I was the worst child she had, I loved her as much as any of her other children. I needed God to restore her strength. Determining in my heart that when God restored her this time, he would also restore the oneness we once had. I believed the Lord was going to work things out and resolve all problems. I just knew deliverance was coming if I just remained patient. Never ceasing to pray for Mama, I knew she would pull through.

One morning on my way to school, as I was driving along the expressway the thought came to my mind that God was going to take Mama. I shook myself crying and repenting for even letting the thought cross my mind. I started rebuking the very thought.

A few evenings later when I came in from school, Mama was in the family room sitting on the couch eating sardines and crackers. A few of the members of the church were over that day. I walked in and sat on the couch across from Mama and said, " I want to sit in here with you, too." She smiled and offered me some of the sardines she was eating, which I gladly accepted. Slowly, I felt she was reaching out to me in her own way.

One Sunday, my family and I had come in from seeing James's triplet brother at the hospital. To my surprise, Mama was up and dressed for church. She was actually getting ready to go out the door. I was so happy! There were times she hadn't been able to make it to all the services as usual because she wasn't feeling well. She was smiling when we walked in, asking how my brother-in -law was doing? James began to explain to her his brother's condition.

As Mama sat there talking to us for a moment she paused and looked down at the Fila slippers she had on that my sister Banita had bought her. Looking up at me she said, "Here try this one on. See how comfortable they are?" I was surprised and happy as I slipped my foot inside her shoe. Mama had Cinderella's feet and all her daughters were like the stepsisters. Ha! Ha! I was happy, because Mama was reaching out to me. Yes! I thought. God is surely doing it! Everything is going to be all right! The least form of communication between us meant so much to me.

A few weeks later, early one Sunday morning as everyone was getting ready for church. I walked downstairs to Mama's house to see how she was doing and to tell her I was about to go. She was sitting in the family room in the rocking chair. She looked tired. I asked if she was all right. She nodded, "yes." Then I told her we were about to go to church, and again she nodded her head "yes", looking up at me. I was disturbed but I went on to church anyway, silently praying in my heart.

After the afternoon broadcast that Sunday, I began to lead the congregation into a praise service. I told them I was doing a victory dance for my mother. Yet after the praise service was over, I felt compelled to go home. Using the excuse that I was going home to cook, I left church. I really just wanted to be near Mama. After I arrived home, I went into Mama's kitchen to prepare dinner, just so I could be near her. She was sitting in the family room on the couch across from the kitchen. I just wanted to be in her presence without being a burden.

Later on that night after everyone had come in from church and gone to bed, two of the church members were sitting downstairs with Mama praying. I had come downstairs with my baby D'Angelo to fix James' lunch for work. After I finished, I felt an urge to remain downstairs and pray with Mama and the others. And so I did, until D'Angelo decided to go upstairs and get into mischief. I began to hear all kind of noises over my head so I decided to go upstairs and put him to sleep. In the process I fell asleep beside him.

What must have been just a few hours later, I was awakened by my daughter Tefa, who was saying, "Momma, they said come move your car, the ambulance is here." I jumped straight up.

Fear covered me as I ran down the steps. Just as I hit the first floor my godmother passed me on her way down to the basement. She was silently weeping. Tears streamed down her face. Fear clutched my heart. My thoughts were racing. Oh God, what is it?

As I stepped into the family room I saw one of the church members sitting on the couch praying. Two others were standing up looking towards Mama. Mama was sitting up on the couch with two of my sisters standing beside her. She had her hand to her chest breathing heavily saying, "I can't breath." I felt so hurt and helpless. Everything seemed to be moving in slow motions except my thoughts that were saying, "Oh my God, what is happening?

At that moment the paramedics came in asking every one to clear the room so they could see about Mama. They seemed to be getting upset because nobody was moving. Finally I said, "Come on you all, move." I didn't want them to get upset with us and take it out on Mama. She had two of my sister's by her side, I knew they weren't going to leave her. I wished to God even then that I were one of those standing near her. My heart ached.

Feeling confident that everything would be all right, I slowly walked up the steps into the girls' room and sat on the foot of the bed praying. I was trying to figure out God's plan. So I said, "All right Lord, maybe you're about to send her to the hospital for a reason, I thought other than for herself. Your ways are pass finding out, maybe someone needs a miracle." Whatever the situation, I trusted God to deliver her.

Some of you might not understand why I thought that way. Let me explain. Mama never went to the hospital for anything, ever since she was called into the ministry. She always trusted God for deliverance!

Since she had become a preacher, the only times she ever went to the hospital was for childbirth. Also Mama had a **REAL** faith and healing ministry. I had actually seen God work through her life many, many times. Therefore, what I knew and what I was seeing seemed to be in conflict. Now I hope you can understand my confusion.

By now I realized everything had become silent. I no longer heard voices. I jumped up and ran into the family room. Everyone had left. I ran and got my coat and jumped into one of the cars. The ambulance had pulled down the street to the corner sitting there for approximately twenty minutes. We were getting upset because of the delay. The paramedic said they had to do the proper protocol. We all sat impatiently waiting to follow them to the hospital.

By the time we made it to the hospital other family and church members were already there. Some were sitting around praying quietly. Others were pacing the halls, quietly waiting, inwardly praying and believing God, not knowing what to expect.

Never in a thousand years did we expect to hear these words, as the doctor came out gathering everyone and saying; "We lost her, I don't know why. She was in perfect health, I'm sorry." I cannot put into words the shock, hurt, anger, and pain that followed. I shall never forget that day as long as I live.

Mama's grandchildren suddenly went into a rage, screaming and crying, walking up and down the hospital corridors and out into the parking lot. My oldest living brother Charles went into an instant rage, crying and hollering, "Mama no, Mama no," God not my Mama!" My dad was standing there trying to comfort Charles.

As I walked a little further down the hall I passed my daughter Tefa, whom Mama had raised. She was crying so uncontrollably. One of James brothers walked over to her and rebuked her sharply, telling her to shut her mouth and pull herself together, because Mama wouldn't want us to carry on like that. Although I didn't say anything, I instantly became angry. I didn't have the strength to respond, but in my mind I wondered, "How can people be so ignorant?" I don't care how religious you are, only God can heal the wound and lift the grief when he decides to take your mother. Lord, help your people.

I could see so many things happening at one time and yet it couldn't be real. No, this was not happening. Somebody wake me up please! Nooo God! Things were not supposed to end like this. My mind seemed to be doing a hundred things at once. Still I was trying to grasp the reality of the situation.

As I made it to the sitting area I saw all my sisters except for Sharlette, sitting around as if in another world. She was standing against the wall not uttering a sound. Janice looked as if she had gone into total shock, staring straight up to the ceiling. My oldest sister Clara was sitting on the other side of the room praying quietly, "Lord, what are we gonna do now?" I could here her murmuring this prayer over and over.

Slowly I walked into the room where they had Mama laying upon the bed, covered up to her neck with a white sheet. Fran was leaning over Mama's body asking God to give her back. My baby sister, Banita, stood on the other side of the bed crying softly with tears streaming down her cheeks. I walked over to the bed silently praying in conjunction with Fran. I felt if God would raise up Mama through anybody's prayers, it would be Fran's, because that she had a gift for fasting and consecration. I figured anytime you can go on a ten or fifteen day fast you should be able to raise the dead and anything else God would have you to do. I honestly believe that. Of course, if it's God's will.

After standing there a while I kissed Mama's forehead, not understanding why she wanted to leave me. Slowly and silently walking out of the room, fighting to hold back the tears, I was yet hoping this was just a bad dream. There were others waiting to see Mama. Perhaps they too were hoping she would rise up. It took a long time for me to realize that once the Lord takes one of His servants home, they don't want to come back.

Those of us who had the strength to function took care of the funeral arrangements, which ended up being my oldest sister Clara, my godmother and myself. I had to make all of the phone calls to tell our relatives and friends the tragic news. Only God could have given me the strength to do that. Some of the people

45

I called went into hysterics, which only seemed to intensify my pain. Still I had to be strong. I had to try to encourage them.

By God's grace we made it through Mama's funeral services. They were held at Monument Of Faith Church in Chicago. Mama was laid out in a beautiful white, gold trimmed casket. Dressed in a white suit trimmed with rhinestones around the lapel, she looked so peaceful.

Mama had approximately fifty grandchildren who formed a choir called the Second-Generation. Her six daughters, Fran, Clara, Sharlette, Janice, Benita and me were all dressed in white rhinestone trimmed suits, identical to Mama's. The daughters sang a song Mama used to sing, "The Last Mile of the Way" and eulogized her home going. My three brothers, Charles, Carlton, and Raymond, who was also dressed in white, sat in the second row next to my Dad, along with a host of other relatives and friends from far and near.

The only way to describe that service is to say it was a miracle. There was a mixture of praises and tears. We were blessed to make it through it. I knew what my sisters must have been feeling, but we knew we had to be strong. We had often been taught not to weep as those that have no hope. So for the sake of our children and the entire church we fought hard to put on expressions of strength.

After the service, we went to the cemetery. It was very cold; blankets of snow were everywhere. Upon reaching the plot, where Mama was to be buried, everyone got out of their cars and gathered around. I can barely remember the prayers and final words spoken by one of the ministers as all eyes rested upon the casket. Everything was like a dream as my eyes swept across the crowd of expressions. Many eyes were filled with silent tears, others were stares of unbelief, and some still seemed shocked. As the casket was lowered into the ground the dream was more like a nightmare of reality. Mama was really gone.

Personally, I felt as if I were literally dying, as if someone had snatched the world from underneath me. I cannot put into words the transition my body went through. I wanted to tell somebody so bad, but I couldn't. Those first couple of days afterwards I felt like death was upon me.

One night in particular after everyone had fell into an exhausted sleep. I was sitting upstairs in my bedroom. This strange sensation that I had begun to feel since Mama's death, came over me. I was too afraid to lie down, afraid this thing would overtake me. So I sat up in the rocking chair that I had in my bedroom, praying quietly, hoping it would soon go away, yet it lingered. All of a sudden I felt my breath getting short. Fear covered me. I was actually trembling, scared, so very scared. I began to repent, begging God to spare my life at least for my children's sake.

I actually thought God was angry with me, punishing me because things were not fully mended between Mama and me prior to her death. I began to beg Him for mercy!

Suddenly I jumped up and ran downstairs and went into the girls' room where my sister Fran was laying across the bed asleep. I wanted to awaken her so badly, yet I was too frightened. As my eyes adjusted to the semi-darkness, I noticed that there were others lying around in there, too. How I longed just to be able to sleep. I was too afraid to even close my eyes. After standing there a moment trying to decide what to do, I sat on the edge of the bed near Fran, praying quietly, telling myself this was not really happening. Yet, I could feel it so real. I knew I couldn't go back upstairs. I knelt beside the bed and began to try to focus on God. Why was He letting this happen to me? Eventually I must have fallen off to sleep.

Over the next few days that feeling of death would come and go. Still I told no one. Sometimes I would close up in my bedroom alone and fight to pray. Other times I would go and sit around my sisters for some sort of comfort, never revealing my turmoil. After awhile, through my constant praying, this feeling finally let up. There were times I could feel it trying to return. I stayed before God, pleading and rebuking death, until one day God brought me complete deliverance.

For days, weeks, and months after Mama's death, I wept bitterly. Every passing day I cried for my Mama. I found it so hard too accept that this had actually happened, worst of all that this was God's will. Why? Why? I cried daily. I spent many sleepless nights telling God, "You didn't fix things before you took her." I wanted every thing to be made right. Sure, she had begun to reach out to me, but I wanted *everything* to be worked out. I wanted that real closeness back! More than anything I wanted her here. I wanted God to give Mama back! I even prayed that He would. I knew He could raise the dead. By any means necessary, I wanted her back! I had begun to have dreams everyday, sometimes one right after the other. In those dreams, Mama would be smiling and talking to me, at times offering me something. At the end of each dream she would tell me to go and do something or she would be preparing to go somewhere. Just before I would go to do what she asked or before she would leave, I would turn and grab her pleading, "No, you're going to leave me." Many times I would drop to my knees crying so hard. When I awaken I would still be crying. For a long time I continued to have those types of dreams from which I would awake so heavy hearted. My mind still hadn't come to grips with the fact that Mama had actually left me.

Another thing that blew my mind was the night I was sitting in my bedroom on the floor looking at Mama's picture, when all of a sudden this thought came to my mind. Just as it came I uttered it out loud. "Mama! How am I going to survive in this marriage without you?" When the realization of what I had just said hit me, I begin to cry. My body trembled as I wept uncontrollably. I had lived 19 years of my life for my mother and now she had lived her life and had gone and left me. It was all so unfair. I loved my mother more than my very own life.

CHAPTER 5

A STRANGER IN MY OWN HOUSEHOLD

As time went on everybody seemed to be moving on but me. I couldn't seem to get a grip on reality. Life was so unfair and unreal. The guilt of not making total amends with Mama before she died was more than I could bear. Nightly I knelt beside her picture weeping, repenting, and begging for forgiveness. I couldn't believe God let it end like this. The guilt was killing me.

About three weeks after God called Mama home, I was yet struggling trying to cope with the grief. I thought maybe if I could see the video tapes of her home-going I could get some sort of relief or comfort. I went and asked my brother-in-law, Frank, Janice's husband, if I could see the videotapes of the services. He said, "No", he wanted to see them first and that he wanted to edit them or something of the sort. I was hurt, but I waited and later on I went and asked him again, explaining to him that I didn't care if the tapes were edited or not. I just needed to see them. Again he said "No."

A few nights later I asked for the keys to Mama's car where I figured he had placed the tapes. I went out to the car, got the tapes and took them into the house. It wasn't long before Janice and Frank figured out what I'd done. They were angry with me. Can you believe it? Janice walked into my bedroom and asked, "Where are the tapes?" I replied, " I've got them." "Give them to me," she said. "No," I answered "If Frank would have let me see the tapes when I asked him in the first place, I wouldn't have taken them."

Janice went back across the hall into her bedroom. Frank sent her back to me again to ask for the tapes. This time she said "Neacie, give me *my tapes.*" "Your tapes?" I said, "She was my mother too!" I couldn't believe my ears. They were acting as if I weren't even a part of this family. As if somehow I was going to destroy those tapes or even worse, I didn't deserve to see them. Janice made a statement about my taking the tapes out of the house because I was into broadcasting. She actually thought I was going to do something to those tapes. Not only was I hurt, but now I had become angry. "I'm not giving you anything," I said. "And don't you let your husband send you back in here again to ask me for nothing, and I mean it!" Upset with me she went out for the second time.

I walked out of my bedroom and proceeded down the hall. Just as I passed their bedroom door Frank called out my name. I kept walking. He called me again. I angrily told him I felt like what he was doing was stupid, and I didn't want to hear it. By the time I made it to the top of the stairs Frank was behind me, shoving my back against the wall, blocking me from going downstairs, and demanded that I listen to him. As I tried to get pass, Frank pushed me again. I knocked his hand off of me. "Look," I told him, " you've got one wife, and don't you ever put your hands on me again."

By that time my sister Sharlett heard the commotion and was coming up the steps. "Take your hands off of her," she said. "She doesn't have to listen to you." At that moment Janice and James were standing in the doorway looking on. Janice, finally speaking up, said to Frank, "Forget it, just leave her alone." She placed her hand on his arm and pulled him away. James just stood there, never uttering a word. Frank stared angrily down at me, breathing heavily, then finally turning and walking away.

The next day word about the incident had gotten around to Fran and Clara. A meeting was called. They asked Frank what was the problem? Why he did not want anyone to see those tapes until he saw them first? Frank gave the same lame excuse about wanting to edit them. I found out other people had asked to see the tapes and he told them no also.

What Frank failed to realize is that this was *my mother* and not his. From what I figured the man had a problem. I didn't care about his reasons. I just made it clear that I never wanted his hands on me again. He apologized. From that day to this, things were never the same between the two of us. I forgave him, but I could never feel that family closeness that we once had. He had wounded me at the worst time of my life. I felt like Mama hadn't been deceased three weeks and he was trying to take over already, just like she said he would. This reminded me of the times when Mama would talk to Janice and me. She would say; "If anything ever happens to me, Frank is going to try and take over." Her words had surely come to pass.

Weeks had turned into months and I was still trying to come to terms with Mama's death. I felt like I was drowning. Everyday the pain only seemed to increase. It hurt so bad, I felt lost. God took the one person that meant the whole world to me. I wished he'd taken me instead. Why couldn't it have been me?

Finally, not knowing what else to do, I asked to talk to all my sisters together. I began to try to explain to them what I was going through. I was reaching out to them for help. I literally asked for their help. I needed them. They sat there quietly listening to me. I don't recall any of them saying anything. When Eloise, the young lady that was practically raised with us, walked in while I was talking, she asked if she could say something. They told her "Yes." I really didn't know what she was about to say. Actually I thought she was out of place, considering I wanted to talk to *my sisters* only. She wasn't really a part of this family. What could she possibly have to say? I was soon about to find out.

At first, I couldn't believe my ears as this woman sat there. She began talking about how Mama rejected me and the things I did. I began to think to myself, *Oh God! I don't need this now.* I was already hurting and confused. After sitting and listening to her for a few minutes, I was so shaken. I got up and went downstairs into the basement. I must have sat down there for at least twenty minutes as this woman elaborated on to the attentive ears of my sisters. I could vaguely hear some of the things she was saying. I sat there trying to blot it out. Why was she doing this?

51

What amazed me was the insight she had on my life, when in actuality this woman hardly came to church when Mama was living. Now she had the revelation. As thoughts ran through my head, my heart felt like somebody was squeezing the breath out of me. Fear covered me. Lord, what's next? Will it ever end?

Eventually I heard one of my sisters calling my name. Slowly I dragged up the steps, my legs feeling like lead. The pain was sapping my strength. After I stepped into the kitchen, they were all sitting around the table. Eloise was standing in the middle of the floor where she had just finished giving her revelation concerning me. I was told I was wrong for walking out. Janice spoke up saying, "Eloise is as much as Mama's daughter as we are and what she said was right." Whatever Eloise said, Janice stood behind her one hundred percent.

After being reproved I knelt down at Eloise's feet and repented. Still in my heart I couldn't believe that in my weakest moment, while trying to reach out for help, my sisters felt led to listen to someone tear me down. I don't remember Fran and Clara saying anything, but Janice let me know she was definitely standing behind Eloise.

From that moment on Janice clung to Eloise. You hardly saw one without the other. To make matters worse, although Clara and Fran were the next two in line in the ministry, Janice actually ran the show. I knew I didn't stand a chance. Janice's revelation was, if the Pastor didn't forgive you, then God didn't forgive you. No matter how many times I went to the altar and repented, every time Janice conducted the service she left me without a ray of hope.

In addition to that Eloise became a prophetess over night. I realize God can use whom He will whenever He will. But every time this woman opened her mouth to prophesy God was angry and wanted to kill the whole church. This woman would prophesy at least five nights straight in a week. Nothing but damnation! Things were really getting scary. To be honest, I had a hard time believing this was God. Why would He take my mother, the Pastor, and then declare utter destruction upon the entire congregation?

One Sunday in the midst of the afternoon service, Janice stood before the church and declared that nothing was going to change. Things must remain like they were when Mama was here. I did not grasp the full intent of her words until later.

From that day forward she treated me like an outcast. Still, at times I would try to talk to her, but her answers were always short. I had begun to notice that whenever one of my other sisters would come around, she could laugh and talk freely with them, but when it came to me she had no time to be bothered. That's when I realized what those words, "nothing was going to change," really meant. Since Mama had pushed me away, Janice felt she must do the same. Mama had created a monster.

I had become a reproach to this family. I thought with my sisters and me sharing the same pain and loss, we would put aside our differences and pull together. We didn't and this hurt me the worst. To them, I was a soul in distress. I was left at a disadvantage because things were not mended between Mama and me.

If only they knew how much I needed them. I needed to know that they still loved me. The rejection was killing me in every way possible. I wanted to die.

THE BITTER YEARS

All ready filled with hurt, pain, confusion and guilt, dear, Righteous Sister Janice managed to provoke me to add on bitterness and anger to my daily companions of emotions. As of this very day, without going into details, I'll say that our relationship went from sisters, best friends, to Jacob and Esau. I'm the one God hates. She's the one He loves. Out of all five of my sisters Janice has managed to treat me like a piece of trash, like an outcast, unworthy of that household or ever to be a part of that ministry again.

53

Even though Janice and I lived in the same household, there was no communication between us. Because of her, her children felt superior to mine and mistreated them, often telling them what they had and what we didn't have. Her oldest daughter resented me without cause. Then again maybe she did have a cause. How could you love someone your own mother doesn't love? Like mother, like daughter.

At that point in my life I was physically, emotionally and mentally drained. I no longer had the will nor strength to fight for the love of my family. I realize that even now I will never be fully accepted by my sisters. I can never be one of them, yet I am.

No longer can I face their stares of pity or resentment. I'm sorry for all the hurt, shame, and pain that I brought to this family. I apologize for not being able to be the wife to the husband chosen for me, which has been the root of all my problems, eventually costing me the love and trust of my family. Worst of all, it caused me the most valuable relationship in the world, my mother and I.

Today I feel my sisters are holding the fact that Mama pushed me away against me. After Mama's home-going, my nieces and nephews would come around and repeat some of the statements my sisters made regarding Mama and me. The one I will never forget is when they said I never came around when Mama was sick. That was a lie. Everyday I made it a point to inquire about her when I first came in the door. Unfortunately, they weren't present so it doesn't count.

I marvel that my sisters have forgotten the confusion of mind when Mama would push them back and they wanted to be with her, but didn't know what to do in order to regain her acceptance. Each one of us has experienced this. It never ceases to amaze me how they have all the answers for me, as to how and what I could or should have done, yet during their trials, like myself, they couldn't find the answers.

Still, time and time again my sisters Clara and Janice felt led by God to stand before the whole church and defame my name across the congregation. I can't speak about everything, but I can definitely say one thing hasn't changed, their opinions and judgments of me.

The last sermon I heard on the last Sunday I appeared in church there, one of my sisters was up preaching. Again, I was the topic: "The unruly wife whose husband needed to put her in line. Let the church say Amen!" According to them, I was going to hell for telling people my mother took away my childhood and made me live saved, a statement I never made. Lord, if they didn't get anything else, they surely got that part of the mantle. They definitely knew how to tear you down, in the name of the Lord. I must inject one thing; "nobody made me live saved." I'm saved because I love God.

I wish to God that my sisters knew my daily struggle, my inward pain. They had no need to constantly keep me at a distance, shun me and verbally beat me down. My inward turmoil was already doing me a job. To make matters worse, I was helping them beat me down. I couldn't seem to shake the guilt concerning the estranged relationship between Mama and me. Sometimes I actually felt like I was going to lose my mind.

Unfortunately, two years after my precious mother's home-going, I was still in that same predicament. In my sisters' eyes, God still hadn't forgiven nor accepted me. So, I was just a bench member whenever I would go to my Mama's church. I got to where I seldom attended church there. I got tired of being the topic of failure and the object of pity and doom. It's a sad thing to say, but I felt better staying at home. The church was supposed to be a healing place, not a killing place.

I was told that this was a test that I must sit and endure until God saw fit to deliver me. Part of it may have been a test, but I definitely felt that my sisters were holding me at fault, and they were waiting on Mama to pay them a visit and tell them when I was all right or delivered. Let them wait. In the mean time, I've decided to try God for myself and move on with my life.

CHAPTER 6

AN OUTCAST AMONG MY OWN

As the next few years went by I became what seemed like a bonafide outcast. I was there and yet not there. The hurt continued. Fortunately I was blessed to remain in college after Mama passed away. I fought to finish my last year toward my degree in broadcasting and communications. I was also working a part time job during the evenings. These were my ways of coping. School and work became my refuge. Still I was under so much pressure; I knew I needed help, yet I pressed on.

Many days at school I would sit in class and zone out, not hearing a word the instructor said. I struggled, having to shake myself at times from the overwhelming thoughts of the troubles I was having at home and at church. I dreaded going home for it was no longer a place where I could receive love and support, or even feel a part of this family. I no longer had a part in anything that was done. More and more I was becoming withdrawn.

No longer did I attend the home prayer meetings, for even in this I felt alienated. The tension in the house was great, yet no one seem to feel it but me. I was the one that was wrong. I was the misfit, the unforgiven soul. This attitude carried from my home to the church. There were still times my name would literally be called out in the church before the entire congregation regarding my marriage and my ungratefulness and that I didn't appreciate the husband of my youth and that he needed to be a man and straighten me out.

Things had gotten to a point where as some of the people in the church would have nothing to do with me. Some of them would not as much as speak.

When special services were conducted and presentations were given, various gifts of appreciation, love, and inspiration would be presented to each one of my sisters, but I was deliberately omitted.

Many times I would be sitting right there either behind or somewhere near my sisters as the saints would march right by me and give them roses, candy and whatever else they had to give. Nevertheless, I kept a straight face, and although I was hurt by this, I wasn't going to give them the satisfaction of knowing it.

I remember so clearly one incident. If I'm not mistaken, it was during one of the memorial services for Mama. That particular night while sitting in church, as the service began, I casually started looking around. As I glanced around I noticed that my sisters where all dressed alike in nice red and black suits. My first impression was how nice they looked; my second thought was the fact that they had not included me, not even to tell me they had planned to dress alike for Mama's service. To add salt to the wound, I noticed Eloise was also dressed like my sisters and so was Mama's adopted daughter Rose. This was not a coincidence.

In every way possible they were making a point. Yes, I was hurt. Still I sat through the remainder of that service as I had through the others. I felt like a spectacle; I knew the congregation had noticed what was going on. Some even walked up and asked me why I wasn't dressed like my sisters, I had no comment.

No matter what was said or done, I felt an obligation to be there and endure such foolishness. The sad part about it all is that they felt justified; they believed this was acceptable unto God.

There were other instances that drove me into further depression and stress. **My family had a way of controlling you or making you feel totally lost.** Daily I lived in fear. My only relief was when I would go to school or work, places where no one could hurt me or try to look down on me. Actually it was the total opposite; other people outside of my church and family seemed to look up to me. Many of them would come to me for advice or even counseling.

I often wondered to myself, how could I help them when my own world is crumbling? Yet I would try. Just helping others seemed to give me an inner strength, a sense of self worth. At that point in my life I had no self-esteem, no belief in myself, and I was wondering, *what is God's role in all of this?*

The pain and confusion were wearing me down. Not only was I suffering mentally and emotionally, but things were now affecting my physical being. All of this was putting more of a strain on my marriage. It was no secret that my family felt like I was my husband's downfall, which was very confusing, since they said God ordained this marriage. So why would God give him someone to destroy him? Nothing was making sense any more. Now I was even responsible for James' shortcomings, and causing my children to go to hell. I was in a no- win situation. I couldn't help my family or myself and God was letting these things continue.

Inwardly and spiritually I was dying as others were assisting my death. There was no hope for me. Through all of this I kept trying to pray, many times not knowing what to say. Often kneeling down or sitting flat on the floor, all I could say was "Oh Jesus," I no longer had the strength to pray a complete prayer. I couldn't seem to find the words to say, no more than "God you already know what I'm trying to say." So many times I would just sit there with tears streaming down my face, wondering, *God how long?* I was tired, so very tired. I could feel myself becoming numb. I prayed that the numbness would continue; it was better to feel nothing than the constant pain.

Late one night as I came home from work I noticed Clara's and Fran's vehicles parked out in front of the house. Considering it was after midnight I knew something was up. *Oh God,* I thought, *not again.* I had a gut feeling that they had come there for me. Right then and there is when I decided I wouldn't attend another counsel meeting. This had to stop. Upon making that decision in my mind and heart, I climbed out of the car and walked into the house, walking right past them without as much as a glance, going straight up stairs to my bedroom. Still they sent for me.

Inwardly I rebelled, but then I calmed down. Silently praying for strength, I slowly walked out of my bedroom and went downstairs where the others were waiting. James and my daughter, Tefa were brought into this meeting also. I walked in and sat down, listening patiently as they began to discuss the things they felt were a problem. Finally after listening to the conversation, going back and forth for a while, I raised my hand and asked if I could say something.

After receiving permission, I proceeded calmly and spoke directly to my sisters. I told them each of us were aware of the problems and conflicts that had arisen in the house since Mama's death. I spoke concerning a few things that were done which hurt me, and because they were done in front of my children, caused them to rebel. But yet and still I was the problem. I was a soul in distress, but when I reached out for help no one was there to help me.

I challenged them to see the situation reversed. I would have been there for each one of them. My sisters sat there silently as I told them, "This family has hurt me for the last time. I'll never give you the opportunity to hurt me again." At that point I needed inner healing, something they didn't really teach. I told them I was sorry I couldn't walk out of there that night and say everything was going to be all right. They had wounded me beyond repair.

Nevertheless, I would take the blame. Not only that, but after I graduated, I would be moving out. I didn't want anything from them. I felt that God would bless me with the things I needed and make a way for me to take care of my children. My desire was to leave the place where I was obviously not wanted. Enough was enough.

When I finished talking to them Clara said she was sorry I felt that way, claiming that everything in that house was as much mine as everybody else's. I knew those were just words. I also knew that they thought I was just saying something when I said I would soon be moving out. I couldn't leave, I had no where to go, or so they thought. Yet I knew once I made that decision I had to act upon it. I would not give them the pleasure of feeling like they were my only hope.

PUTTING AN END TO THE MADNESS

That was the last meeting for me. After that I basically went into my own world, just my children and me. I didn't feel like I owed any one else anything. Sure, I was still living with my family, but I no longer tried to win their acceptance or approval. I had become numb where they were concerned, shutting down all emotions. I learned to love them at a distance, avoiding them in every way possible, attending church only on Sunday's and for special services to support my children. Slowly but surely I grew away from my family.

Through all of this I felt like I was finally growing up, more than I had felt in all the years of my life. I was fast learning how to be a woman and to stand on my own feet. Thank God I always had my own mind. I continued working hard to finish school while working two part-time jobs to have some money to help take care of my children. The thoughts and opinions of my family were now in the background. There had to be a better life for me. Every now and then my family would manage to get in a dig by making negative or discouraging comments, but I would grit my teeth and bare the pain. Unknown to them I was learning not to react to their foolish tactics of control.

Still there was one major problem, the main thing that kept me connected to all of this; my marriage. James and I were still having problems. I wanted to go to counseling outside of our church, he didn't. I wanted to move out of my family's home but he couldn't afford to. Worst of all, I had no desire for him, but I thought we could remain together for the children's sake. After awhile even that thought wore off. I was just plain miserable. Who was I kidding? Why should I continue to torture myself by remaining in a marriage that was draining the very life out of me? Although I cooked James' meals and washed his clothes, I couldn't stand to be in the same room with him. I had begun to attend other churches; James remained at my mother's church. This was fine with me except for the fact he didn't believe we could be saved at any other church. I felt sorry for him, yet I realized that sympathy alone was not enough to sustain this marriage.

My family had ruined any chance of my loving James. Because of the guilt they constantly laid upon me, I could only view him as the root of all my problems. I couldn't love him the way my mother did. I quietly resented him, feeling he was the cause of the breach between my mother and me. I went from blaming myself to blaming him, finally to blaming the church.

DO OR DIE

I definitely had to do something about my life because to continue on in this manner would eventually kill me. Although I was doing well in school, my personal life was taking its toll on me. To see me in the classroom or passing in the halls, you would have thought I was one of the happiest persons in the world. On the inside I was miserable, carrying a burden of pain, bitterness, fear, guilt, and God knows what else.

By the grace of God my work-study supervisor at the college, who was a minister, figured something was wrong. Sure he knew I was saved, but still he detected something wasn't right. Finally one day as he was sitting in the office talking to me, without going into specific details, I mentioned the things that were obviously stressing me out. He sat quietly listening. When he spoke he said, "Mary, it is not God's will that the saints should be miserable." After that he had me open one of the Bibles he kept in the office. Then, while going over some scripture passages with me, he told me to pray and ask God for guidance. From then on when he would have a chance to talk to me, he would speak words of life, going over various scripture readings to encourage me, telling me to trust God. Yet I knew in the depths of my soul I had to make a decision. I could either stay in this situation with my marriage and the church or release it all and trust God to help me. I was confused and scared. Maybe my family was right. Maybe God did want me to suffer like this. Lord, what do I do? What is your will? I needed some answers. The stress of it all was causing me to now have physical pain in my chest. Yet I kept going on, trying to endure.

At the beginning of the next semester I had to fill out more forms to continue getting financial aid. This time the financial aid advisor wanted a copy of my marriage license. I couldn't remember ever having a copy. I had only seen it once or twice many years ago. To be perfectly honest I didn't want to see it. It only held sad memories for me.

Anyway after talking to my advisor I had to go downtown to City Hall and obtain a copy of my marriage license. After I filled out the forms, the clerk came back to tell me he couldn't find it. Still he went back again to check under the year before and the year after I was married. Again he returned with nothing. Patiently he tried to help me remember when and where I had gotten married. I told him I was married in Chicago. I gave him the name and location of the church where the wedding took place. That's when it dawned on me. I had had a wedding here but I was actually married in the state of Alabama, a month before the wedding ceremony took place in Chicago. Apologizing, I told him what happened, and in return he gave me the information I needed to obtain my license from Alabama. As I left the building, memories came flooding back. I felt strange.

Within two weeks the document was mailed to me. The day after I received it I went to see my advisor to submit my papers. I handed her my marriage license, and as she began to read it, I cried. Apologizing for my emotional outburst, I briefly explained to her that my marriage had been arranged. Since then I had never seen a copy of my license. She was very understanding. From that day forward she was one of many individuals with whom God had granted me favor. She encouraged and motivated me to succeed, and applauded my every step towards success.

One day while sitting in my work-study supervisor's office alone, the weight of the world seemed to crash down on my shoulders. Tears begin to stream down my cheeks; quietly I began to talk to God. I knew this was it, I had to make a decision that day. The need weighed down heavily upon me. I had cried over this for the last time. I promised God right then and there that I would not allow myself to go through this agony another year. Sink or swim, I knew what I had to do! I dried my eyes, walked over to the computer and began to type a letter to my husband. Regardless of the outcome we both must face the truth. I needed to be honest with him and myself! Although I had mentioned some of these things to James before, in this letter I laid it all out plainly yet gently, stating among other things that this marriage was wrong from the beginning. When things don't start out right they don't end right. For the first time I told him I didn't love him, and I'd never loved him; I asked for a divorce. I requested that he talk to me once he finished reading the letter. I had to be honest with him. I no longer had the strength to pretend.

That evening while sitting at home in the bedroom talking, I gave James the letter. I walked out of the room to give him some privacy and some time to think. When I returned, he was lying across the bed with his face towards the wall. I felt a relief now that the truth was out in the open, but I was slightly afraid of his response. James was so quiet I asked him to tell me what was on his mind. He was shocked. He said he had seen a lot of guys at work go through this, but he never thought it would happen to him. James was hurt. I was so very sorry, but I knew I had made the right decision. I had sought God for guidance. And a great pressure left me once I made that decision. I wasn't trying to hurt him, neither was I insensitive of his feelings. I just knew deep down that this was it for us. Still I didn't want him to be bitter.

For the next few days James didn't have much to say to me. One evening I asked him to talk to me about what he thought and felt. He told me he felt like I had been deceitful with him, and that I should have told him these things a long time ago. He would have let me go then. I tried to explain to him that I couldn't. Had I done this long ago I believed I would have been exiled from the family and the church. I honestly felt Mama wouldn't have wanted anything more to do with me, and even worst she and James would have taken my children, labeling me an unfit mother. I didn't want to lose my children.

Mama had lived her life and had now gone on to be with the Lord. I no longer had a part in the church, my family had distanced themselves from me, and my two oldest children were now adults. I had nothing to lose. James knew I spoke the truth!

A few days later, though I don't recall the entire conversation as we were talking, I'll never forget his words, "your mother said you had a whore's forehead." I instantly became angry, responding, "Don't you ever as long as you live tell me that again. Mama only said that to beat me down with guilt and to keep me confined in this marriage to you!" Then I calmed myself and said, "You're right. You all made a good whore out of me, for only a whore can sleep with a man she has no feelings for. You're right, I've been your whore for over twenty years." James didn't say another word.

The following week I went downtown, got a lawyer, and filed for a divorce. I went back home and talked it over with James. We agreed to talk to the children together. I knew this would be the worse part, but they had to know. All this time my family had my children under the impression that I never appreciated their father, and that their father was the perfect man. Now they would know the truth. Somehow I had to gently tell them about the arrangement of this marriage and how my family controlled it. I hated having to hurt my children, but I needed them to understand. I wasn't the monster I was made out to be.

After gathering my children and telling them the situation, they heard us out, and then pleaded for us to live together but in separate rooms. In spite of the circumstances they loved and wanted the both of us. I thought about it for a while, but I knew that wouldn't work. As long as we were in the same house, James would want me to fulfill my personal wifely duties. I knew I could no longer cater to him. That was out of the question. I understood their hurt but I could only pray that as time went on they would be all right.

My children will always have the both of us although we would no longer be together. My two oldest were twenty-one and eighteen years old. I felt that I had given my children, James, and my family the best years of my life. I spent over twenty-two years in an arranged marriage I had no control over since the tender age of fourteen. Surely I had paid my dues. We all decided to keep silent about the divorce. This was not something I wanted discussed neither among my family nor in front of the entire church. For once I made a decision on my own with only the help of God.

CHAPTER 7

BY THE GRACE OF GOD

By the grace of God on May 15, 1998, I graduated on the dean's list of honor students from Kennedy King College as a broadcast major. I was even blessed to write and sing the graduation song entitled "Oh Kennedy, Oh King, We Love You". Considering all I had been through, this was a big accomplishment for me and one of the most joyous moments of my life.

Still in the midst of my accomplishments I had mixed emotions. I could see the blessings of God upon my life, yet I wondered was this really Him. I was being blessed and rejected at the same time. I received awards at the College's Honor Convocation for my achievements and contributions, but no support or congratulations from my sisters. Not one of them came to my graduation, but I love them just the same. I'm grateful to my brothers, Charles and Carlton for they supported and stood by me in every way possible. My children, the loves of my life, James, and my friends were there to share each special occasion with me. My Dad came also. I appreciate this.

That Monday following my graduation, I moved out of my family's house and moved in with a lady I knew from another church. She offered to take my children and me in until I was stable and back upon my feet. I must admit I was afraid. This was one of the greatest steps of my life. I had never lived away from my family, yet I knew the time had come. If I was to heal from the wounds and scars they had caused, I knew I had to get away. This was the only way to escape the bitterness that was threatening to overtake me.

Strength and courage were now outweighing my fears. Sink or swim, I had to go. Driven by pain and a deeply wounded soul, I packed my belongings, gathered my children and grabbed a hold on the only thing I had left, my faith in God. I launched out for a new beginning.

Knowing I couldn't go back once I left didn't bother me. The fact I knew that some people were waiting for me to hit rock bottom, just to be able to say "I told you so," made me angry. It's disheartening to know church people can be so bitter and vengeful, wanting God to destroy you just so they can be recognized as a true prophet or servant of God.

Nevertheless, I never ceased to pray for them as I pressed on. Bracing myself for the worst, not knowing what to expect from one day to the next, I persevered. It got rough at times, but I had to keep the faith. I had been through too much to disbelieve now. One day it seemed as if I could see my way; the next day it was dim. Yet in the midst of all that, God would always send someone along to help me out one way or the other. From finances to food, the need was met.

Still I knew I could only accept the support of others for so long. It was a must that I continue to fight to stand on my own feet. The fact that I had the courage to break away from my family was a huge step for me, now I must move forward. It was not an easy task.

I kept looking for work while working two part time jobs at two different radio stations as a radio personality. In between that I would get paid for hosting various gospel musicals and festivities, but I needed a full time job in order to provide for my children sufficiently and to have a home for them.

By the time the third month rolled around I had been through many ups and downs, mentally, emotionally, spiritually, and worst of all, financially. I was barely making it. It wouldn't have been so bad if I didn't have four children depending on me. There had to be a better way.

One evening I gathered my children together and told them all we had was one another, and we must pull together. My two oldest had to find jobs and I believed God to bless me with full time work. I figured once we all began to work we could save our money and buy a home. Until then we had to make the best of where we were and what we had.

The next morning I got up and went down to the Public Aid office. Although I didn't know much about this program, I knew pride wouldn't feed my children. Standing in line with hundreds of other people, I prayed that my case would be accepted. I also prayed that I wouldn't see any of the members from my mother's church. That would have been a disaster. I knew they would have felt that since I had left the church, God was punishing me, and now I had to stand in the Public Aid line. Being a pastor's child, this would have been looked at as a disgrace. To me it was a blessing; not only that, but a lesson. Who knows the mind of God?

Nevertheless, I was blessed with a good caseworker, and within the next few weeks I was receiving full benefits of public aid. From there I went to the unemployment office. Again God blessed me with people who worked diligently to help me. In the meantime I kept filling out applications, submitting resumes, and going on interviews. Every step of the way I thanked God that at least we had food in the house provided by Public Aid. If anybody was ever happy for the Link Card, I was a happy soul, but I wasn't about to make a living off of it. I may not be the smartest person in the world, but I have a decent amount of education, talents, determination and a growing confidence that things would get better. They had to; I belong to God.

Not knowing where my life was headed I knew I had to believe God, no matter what. Although I had been wounded so badly in the church, I didn't let that stop me from loving God. I was aching to find a church home. Even though I loved my original church, I knew I couldn't go back. Things would never be the same. To them I was a failure. However I knew a God of the impossible, a God that could turn failure to success, evil into good, and make the wrong right.

The worse my trials became, the stronger my faith was. I had to keep my trust in God. Where could I go? I didn't know why He saw fit to allow my life to go the way it did, but I knew He must have had a plan.

Weary, weak, and worn I sought another church home. It wasn't easy. I kept feeling like there was no other place for me. I felt obligated to stay at my original church home because that was Mama's church and where my ministry had begun. Still I knew the ways of God were past finding out. My way was not his way. God was moving me out of my comfort zone. That was not what I wanted at all! I wanted God to fix things between my family, my church and myself. I wanted them to accept me again and for all my portions in that ministry to be restored. I couldn't believe that God would move me on to another ministry. I cried many days and nights. I fought it in every way possible. Every time I would kneel down to pray, the church that I honestly felt led to go to would linger in my mind, The Monument Of Faith Church.

Down through the years I would always pray for my church and other ministries, but this was different. Every time I would pray for my church, this particular church would linger on my heart so heavy, causing me to weep so bitterly, knowing God was trying to tell me something that I did not want to hear.

This was something I never thought in a thousand years would ever happen to me. I had seen different ones leave their home church for one reason or another, but I always felt not me, I am not the one. I felt like I was one of the pillars of my home church, but evidently God had other plans. I struggled for months. I was determined to remain at my original home church. Things only got worse. No matter what I did, I was not accepted, never restored.

Eventually, I began to attend services at the Monument Of Faith Church, under the leadership of Apostle Richard D. Henton. I would sit through various services with just enough strength to lift my hands and cry, as the people would praise God. I couldn't stand and give a testimony, join any auxiliary, or anything. I needed inner healing. All I wanted was to hear the word of God. I needed to hear words of life. Somehow and

70

some way I needed to know God had not forsaken me, and that there was hope for me. I needed God's love more than I needed to breathe. I longed for the presence of God, to just feel his precious anointing once more, His presence and His spirit.

Many days I felt so strange, as if I didn't know who I was any more. How in the world did I get here? Where was my life going? Yet as time went on I settled myself, asking God to just let me start over. I didn't care about titles. I just wanted the Lord to consider his own one more time. Holding on to one passage of scripture I waited on God. Psalm 51 became my prayer, realizing no matter what the task, only God could reach into this horrible pit and save my dying soul.

Still I battled with questions and confusions. Nothing was making any sense any more. I didn't seem to know what to believe any more. The only part of my life that made any sense was my belief in God. My outlook on some things within the church began to change. I no longer saw people according to their denominations, but they were all souls that belong to God, regardless of their situations or conditions.

I began to understand why God let me suffer certain things. Even in my darkest hour he made my light to shine before others. Every now and then God would open my mind and let me get a glimpse of knowledge. I begin to learn how to encourage myself through the Word of God. Although there are many things I may not ever understand and some questions in my life may never be answered, the Lord didn't leave me clueless.

Now I had begun to understand that my trials would be someone else's triumph. My pain was not in vain. God had a definite plan for my life. I wasn't sure of where he was actually taking me or how far, but I knew the God that had begun a good work in me was able to complete it. Though I had a glimpse of what was to come, skepticism had a way of over shadowing me.

The Lord would allow different ones at different times to tell me the same thing concerning my ministry. God was preparing me for something great. I didn't run from church to church

71

looking for a prophecy. God knows I don't believe everything people prophesy. I don't play with God, and I'm very careful in that area. Nor did I go to churches looking for someone to give me a word. As far as I'm concerned we have 66 books worth of words in the Bible. The Lord had a way of speaking to me through the least one of His little ones, from people that knew me to others who didn't.

Eventually as my healing began to take place, I became more active within the church. Over a period of time some of the same portions I had in my mother's ministry was offered to me at the one I now attend. Still I was hesitant. I treaded carefully. I had to know God's will and acceptance for my life. I had been wounded too badly to take anything for granted. Yet I know the Lord has no pleasure in the soul that draws back. It was time for me to let go of the past and move forward. I once heard a preacher say, "After God has been good enough to bring you out, then you ought to be grateful enough to let it go." That's one statement I never forgot. I took that message very personally. Once I made that decision, I could see God working in my favor.

Not many days hence the Lord blessed me with a new job, the best job I ever had in my entire life other than my ministry. He blessed me with an excellent supervisor with whom the Lord granted me favor. He placed people in my life that believed in me and admired the call upon my life.

Slowly but surely I grew to feel free and love my present church home, Monument Of Faith. Step by step my life began to fall into line. The ministry I once had and longed for once again began to prosper. Now I understood what the minister meant when he said, thank those who have wounded and mistreated you, for they had actually done you a favor. Their rejection of me only caused me to believe and trust God the more. I had to depend on Him. I had no other choice. The Lord put things in such a way; no one could fix them but Him. As the words to the song goes that I sometime sing with the Voices of Monument, "there's nobody like Jesus!"

Through the worse trials in my life, when I just knew I wasn't fit or worthy of God's goodness, He took the evil and turned it into good. I couldn't pray, as I desired. I didn't have the strength to fast, yet I kept asking God to remember me not according to my righteousness, for surely as the scripture says, they were as filthy rags.

The 7th chapter of the book of Matthew and the 7th verse that states: Ask and it shall be given; seek and you shall find; knock, and the door shall be opened unto you, and that everyone that asketh, receiveth. This is the scripture in which my strength lie.

I begin to say to God, "Lord you didn't say we had to be perfect or even righteous to receive that promise. Please do it for me just because you said it, and because I need it so badly." I needed a restoration in every way possible, spiritually, mentally, emotionally, and financially. If ever I needed God to consider his promise, I needed it then.

Somewhere in the midst of all that, God heard my cry. I could begin to see the light at the end of the tunnel. It took some time, but my healing and deliverance had begun. In the face of total adversity my God had once more remembered me and enabled me to make the ultimate comeback. When man said, "I wouldn't," God said, "I will." And I'm telling you He did it! It was a long uphill journey, but I made it by the tender mercies and grace of God. To God be the Glory forever!

CHAPTER 8

HIS STORY

I am sure many of you wonder how James feels, and what was his point of view. I will tell you his side of the story in his words to the best of my ability to remember.

One day while sitting in a restaurant having a conversation I told James I needed to talk about our situation. I wanted to know how he allowed himself to be put into this type of situation, considering he was of age during the time. His response was that during the time he had gotten saved, he had recently broken up with the young lady he'd brought to church with him, to whom he was engaged. After that happened, he figured he would just seek God and travel with the ministry until the Lord saw fit to send him a wife.

One day James was talking to the Pastor, who was my mother, and during that conversation he mentioned he was a virgin. Of course she was surprised. It is not every day you find a twenty-three year old man who is still a virgin. She thought this was commendable. After that James said he noticed she had begun to preach about virgins a lot.

Many times the Pastor would talk to him and share different scripture readings concerning virgins, which he said made him feel special. More and more the topic of virgins was elaborated upon across the pulpit. One day my mother told him that because he was a virgin, he could choose to marry anybody he wanted. Of course it would be better if he chose another virgin.

Not long after that the Pastor called him into the church office. She told him that while she was sitting in the pulpit, the Lord had spoken to her and told her that he was going to be her son-in-law. She said in her mind she was wondering how? Which one of her daughters was he going to marry? The two oldest were already married and the next two were already spoken for. The only two left were the two youngest, Banita and me, and we were too young.

Then she told him I was mature for my age and that he could marry me. He was shocked. He replied; "she's too young!" "She's more mature than you think," mother answered. "I didn't talk to girls I thought were too young before I was saved," he protested. Nevertheless she kept talking to him, and as he sat there listening, he began to think within himself, "She is nice looking, and her mother did say she liked me. Maybe I can talk to her." Afterwards he said he was excited about the thought of getting married, and marrying a nice looking young girl.

Right after that, through mother's persuasion, he came to talk to me. By that time she had already spoken to me and told me I *had* to marry him. When he approached me, I told him, "I don't like you, and I don't want to marry you, but since the Pastor said it's God's will, I will. Just let me finish school first." End of conversation.

Of course James went back to my mother and told her what I had said. Still Mama, along with Sharlett, assured him that I did like him and that was how virgins were supposed to act. He knew my father and my oldest sister Fran were against it, and in their own way they made it known to him. As for the rest of my family, after mom explained things to them they neither spoke for or against it. From then on James said, "I was walking on air!"

Because of what he was constantly told to do and what he felt, he never considered my real feelings.

CHAPTER 9

A REAL AWAKENING

As I take a quick review of my life, I must say I've had a real awakening. I speak concerning some of the things I endured, thinking I was doing God a service. As I grew older, the more things I went through, the more my understanding became enlightened. By now you must know I'm speaking about my marriage, which I entered into under the instruction that this was God's will. If I didn't consent I would go to hell.

Unfortunately, it took a very long while but eventually God opened my eyes to the truth of the matter. Deep within my heart as I grew older I knew the truth but couldn't risk losing the things I valued. My Mother's love, my church, and my family. Those were the things that caused me to live over 22 years of my life miserably. In a situation I never wanted, was never happy with, and never really understood, believing I was doing God a favor.

Nevertheless, the sacrifice was not in vain. Perhaps my story can be the revelation not just for the women and young girls in the church, but all little girls and women in foreign countries and through out the world, who are living under such customs and religious traditions.

I realize now that a lot of things that were said to me and the way in which I was treated was nothing but mind control. Things that were supposed to be for the benefit of my soul such as, spiritual guidance, admonishing, exhortation and correction, at times, caused me more hurt than help.

Others needed to remind me of my short-comings and make me feel guilty all the time for my lack of emotions. I developed a fear of becoming a failure, often feeling guilty because I wasn't happy with my situation or the way it was going. Those were tactics used to keep me in a marriage of confinement.

It has been said that happiness is a state of mind. But how could my mind be happy when it was confused and unstable. Why would God put me in a predicament that he knew I never wanted or would never be content in?

TO UNDERSTAND AND FORGIVE

Before God delivered me I had reached a point of bitter resentment. I was angry, hurt, confused, scared and depressed. I wanted help, but I felt like there was no one I could trust. Every time I felt a desperate need to go to some one, there was always a greater reason why I shouldn't. I was so afraid of rejection. I felt like God himself had forsaken me. I had no belief in myself and nothing else. I lived in a constant state of wonderment, no confidence and very low self-esteem.

Day after day I wondered, pleading with God. Why? I became withdrawn from everybody, most of all my family. Some of them I resented for putting me through such anguish. Worst of all I resented James, for I felt he took my mother's love from me. I shunned all so-called friends. I stopped preaching and singing. My whole life seemed to be on hold.

Until that day, I can't say exactly when. All I know is that when I got away from everything and everybody that was associated with my pain and my past, I begin to seek and trust God. In my darkest hour I held on to my faith. All I had going for me was the promises of God and the fact that I was His chosen vessel. That was the one thing I knew, not even the devil in hell could change. That was my life line, my light at the end of a dark tunnel.

I began to seek God for guidance and understanding. I stayed before God my insight changed. It took a while but finally I no longer resented those I felt had wronged me. Instead of carrying the blame, I prayed for their wellbeing and success. I asked God to strengthen them as he had strengthened me. Not a day passed without me praying for my sisters, that God would enable them to uphold the ministry which he had began through my mother.

I no longer nursed a silent anger for what I felt Mama had wrongfully done. For now I finally understood. Mama did what she honestly felt was for my good. Perhaps she felt if she chose a good husband for me, she wouldn't have to worry about my well-being in the future. The reproofs she often administered were not to wound me but to make me strong.

My greatest regret is that if only Mama would have put her arms around me sometimes and explained those things to me, maybe things would have turned out differently. Mama was not the overall affectionate type. She raised her daughters to be tough. Still I longed for that affection. To be tough is good, but nothing beats a warm embrace.

I'm not saying Mama never showed us any love. Her love was expressed mostly through the things she would do. I guess you can say it was more physical than verbal. She just wasn't the type to say, "I love you just because." Still I love my mother and my sisters more than they will ever know. Even as I print these words, tears fill my eyes and run down my cheeks. Unknown to them, Mama was my hero and my sisters were everything I wanted to be.

Even now I would like to make a final apology to my family. I ask your forgiveness for all things and your love beyond conditions. By the same token, although there are scars that can never be erased, God has taught me how to forgive and continue to love. I realize I must love you, for you are and will forever be a part of me. As Joseph spoke to his brothers Genesis 50:20 "Ye thought evil against me; but God meant it unto good, to bring to pass, as it is this day, to save much people alive."

As for James, I no longer resent him. Now I understand that he was just as innocent as I was through an act of obedience. At first, the first few months after we separated I couldn't stand seeing him. I felt angry because of the guilt my family had instilled in me towards him. Therefore, I felt better when he didn't come around.

Eventually when God began to heal me, I can now see James as a friend and of course respect him as my children's father. There's hardly a time when I kneel to pray that I don't fail to ask God to strengthen James and to heal his broken heart. In spite of everything, I never meant to hurt him. I pray he can find it in his heart to forgive me. Maybe one day after reading this book, he will understand.

CHAPTER 10

TO MY SURPRISE I WAS NOT ALONE

One day I ran into an individual I knew from another church. We began to make polite conversation about our families and churches. During this conversation I mentioned to him that I was writing a book, briefly telling him what it was about. He looked at me with a surprised expression and said that he wanted to talk to me more at another time. He went on to say that he knew someone else that was in a similar situation. I was curious. For so long I thought I was the only one in this day and time in this type of situation.

Throughout the rest of the day I pondered about how many people in the churches across the United States are living in this kind of arrangement?

The next morning I awoke about 5:00 a.m. For some reason I could not go back to sleep. My mind was cluttered with so many thoughts, and memories begin to cloud my mind. It hit me all of a sudden. "Oh my God, it all begin to come back to me." No, I was not the only one.

As I recall, it was a few months after I was married. An announcement was made in the church that Anne, another one of the young girls, was getting married. Anne happened to be one of my best friends. We were both 14 years old. As I sat there listening to the announcement that she was to marry my husband's twin brother Josh, I became so angry.

After the service that night I couldn't wait to get her alone. That's exactly what I did when I thought no one was looking. I called Anne into the back of the church between the two double doors which lead up to the second sanctuary of the church. Then I angrily turned to her and asked her had she lost her mind? I was so upset I tried to talk her out of it.

Mama had always said Anne wanted to be like me. This time I felt she was taking it too far! My God I wasn't even happy with this arrangement. How could I get her to see that without getting into trouble? I knew if my mother found out that I was trying to talk her out of this, I would surely get rebuked! Strangely enough Anne stood there kind of half smiling at me during the whole time I was talking to her. She seemed uncertain. Besides being angry I felt sorry for her. Finally I let her go. I knew our parents would be outside waiting for us. I didn't talk to her much after that. After Anne got married, I resented weddings, they all made me sad.

Over the years Anne adjusted to that sort of arrangement better than I did. I never really heard her complain. I guess she was more like what the Apostle Paul said in the scriptures about learning to be content in whatever state you're in. On the other hand, I guess I was more like the verse that said, "All men can't receive this saying". I hated being in an arranged marriage.

I also remembered another little girl named Candy that was even younger than Anne and I. She was only about 12 years old. Now that I think about, it she married my husband's youngest brother, Carl, whom she left after a couple of years. Did these brothers have a craving for young girls or what?

One night a few years ago, we were all invited to my mother-in-law's house. I can't recall how the conversation started, but Candy told me why she left Carl. She told how he treated her and the things she went through while in that marriage.

As she spoke, I could vaguely remember hearing about the one time Carl whipped her for going outside to play rope with some of the other children. He felt like she should have been in the house behaving like a wife!

My God she was only a child! As Candy shared these things with me, I stood there with mixed emotions. I begin to remember how people criticized her for leaving him, yet I understood her plight. To be perfectly honest I applauded her courage. Nobody can understand these situations unless they've actually lived through it.

In spite the difficulty, Candy learned to make it on her own with just her and her children. Fortunately for Candy, her mother stood by her. Before the conversation ended, I asked her why she married so young. I knew her situation wasn't quite like mine. Candy replied, "I didn't know what I was doing. Everyone was talking about getting married and it sounded exciting. So when Carl asked me to marry him and being persuaded by others, I said yes." To her surprise it was not what she thought it would be. I can't help but wonder what her mother was thinking?

I wasn't as alone as I thought I was. I wonder how many churches have these situations in the midst. I used to wonder if all Christians had to have a miserable marriage to have salvation? It seemed as though the Pentecostal churches hardly had couples marrying for love. Have we become so religious that real love doesn't matter? I think not! I got tired of hearing that line, "You will grow to love him." Why couldn't we love them before we married? That's my opinion. I guess I'm a Pentecostal radical.

HOW DO WE JUSTIFY?

Considering all that has been said and done, now I ask; how do we justify arranged marriages through the scriptures? Is it because in the Old Testament the men could choose their wives without the woman's consent? All they needed was the consent of their families or fathers. According to my understanding women were not highly regarded then. They were to obey, bake bread, and bring forth children. I'm not against the marital responsibilities, but at least marry a man that makes you happy to bake his bread.

Even if we were to seek scriptural reverence to justify such arrangements, lets briefly look into the marriage arrangements of our forefathers, Abraham, Isaac, and Jacob. First there was Abraham at that time called (Abram), Genesis 11:29. And

Abram and Nahor (his brother) *took* them wives: the name of Abram's wife was Sarai.

In the next generation there was Isaac (Abram's son) in the 24th Chapter of Genesis Abraham caused his eldest servant to swear by the Lord that he would go among his kindred and take a wife unto his son Isaac. The servant inquired, "peradventure the woman will not be willing to follow me into this land." To which Abraham responded, "And if the woman will not be willing to follow thee, then thou shall be clear from this my oath." The servant then proceeded on his journey. On the way to find Isaac a wife he sought God for a sign and confirmation. The sign was that the damsel to whom he would say, "Let down thy pitcher, I pray thee, that I may drink; and she shall say, Drink, and I will give thy camels drink also, let the same be she that thou hast appointed for thy servant Isaac." And it came to pass. The confirmation came when it was time for the servant to return to his master Abraham and they sent for the damsel, whose name was Rebekah, asking "Wilt thou go with this man?" And she said, "I will go." In spite of all that took place in between, the final confirmation lied in the response of Rebekah.

Then there's Jacob whom the Bible declares in Genesis 29:10-11. And it came to pass, when Jacob saw Rachel the daughter of Laban his mother's brother, and the sheep of Laban his mother's brother, Jacob went near, and rolled the stone from the well's mouth, and watered the flock of Laban his mother's brother. And Jacob kissed Rachel, and lifted up his voice and wept. That was love at first sight. And as we continue the story we learn of the dedicated love Jacob had for Rachel, which was proven through the things he endured.

And so the Bible lets us know that even then the women had a choice in the matter. If a man tells you the Lord says you're his wife, then trust me the Lord will give you (the woman) a sign also. If the minister or those in authority says God has chosen a special someone for you, then God will give the both of you a sign of confirmation. There's no greater sign then when two hearts are on one accord.

Nevertheless regardless of tradition, custom or belief, as pre-teens between the ages of 12 and 15, under no circumstances are they prepared for marriage. At that age, most young girls are just getting into womanhood. Perhaps some may feel they are prepared for marriage and it's responsibilities, but at that age or stage in life I believe they yet have some maturing to do.

Besides whatever passage of scripture or spiritual reference you may suggest, I believe that a great part of this is based on some mothers wanting their daughters to marry the type of men they desired to marry, especially in my case. With all their good intentions, they don't have the right to live their lives through their daughter's. As for the daughters, although we love our parents and even mimic them in our life styles and mannerisms, our taste may differ. Parents should try to understand and respect that.

Since God laid it upon my heart to write my story, I have heard so many versions of people living in arranged marriages, marriages in which young people were encouraged and persuaded to marry in order to save their souls from destruction. Some of those marriages were based on the fact that the church or the families felt that certain individuals would make a perfect couple. Some even declared that it's the will of God. Yet a lot of those marriages ended in disaster.

Marriage can be such a beautiful thing if done right according to the will of God. Then it can be the worst commitment in your life, if in the midst of the marriage you're miserable. I find it hard to believe that God ordains situations that He knows will make us miserable. I've seen and heard so much until I find it hard to accept when a man tells a woman, "the Lord said you're my wife." I realize there's an exception to the rule, but trust me it's a very rare exception. And along with that, if the Lord chooses someone for you, then I'm sure he will give you a love for and an attraction to that person.

The Bible clearly states in Ephesians 5:25, "Husbands love your wives, even as Christ also loved the church." The 28th verse says, " men ought to love their wives as they love their own bodies." So if you should ask what's love got to do with it, according to the scripture I would say, everything!

A man once told me he was dating a woman whom he really cared for, and the Lord spoke to him and told him that another woman whom he didn't know, neither was attracted to, was his wife. He went to her and told her what the Lord had said. She rejected him. Still he persisted until she consented. Upon conclusion of his story I asked, "How do you know she loves you?" He looked at me with an expression of utter surprise, stating, "I don't know, I never thought about that." Getting up to leave he looked at me and said, "I'm going home to ask my wife if she loves me."

Will somebody please help me to understand the purpose of putting two people together who have absolutely nothing in common? And even worse, no love or attraction for one another. What's really going on? Is this really God? I am the one person that would really like to know. I lived in an arranged marriage for over 22 years of my life. Even though I fought hard to do the right thing and to please God, I was miserable, completely unhappy. Yet I endured that marriage for the sake of what I had been taught.

Every year as I grew older, more and more I wanted to know, what does God have to do with this? Did He really have to make me this miserable in order to be pleased in my life? That was no easy task. The most important thing about it is that I made it through. When God did deliver me, I still had a portion of my youth and the four greatest inspirations in my life, my four children.

Perhaps there is no justification, but I believe there is a reason for everything. Since writing this book I have come to understand why the Lord allowed me to endure such trauma. Perhaps it was not for me, but for you that have been hurt, are yet hurting, and bound by custom and tradition.

The time has come. God is bringing us into a realm of healing, of our hearts and minds. To all the women and men who have been wounded and bound in these seemingly impossible situations, I encourage you to hold on and trust God. I pass on to you the words endorsed by the legendary gospel artist/preacher, Pastor Shirley Ceasar, "You're next in line for a miracle!"

CONCLUSION

THE HEALING PHASE

What we must realize whether we're Christians or not, healing is not always easy but it is necessary. Healing is just as essential to our hearts, minds, and spirits as it is to our bodies. Anyone who has had to face any sort of trauma in life must go through a process of healing in order to successfully go on to the next phase in their life.

Healing resembles rehabilitation in some forms; it has its relapses and moments of depression. The healing process is an emotional roller coaster. One moment you're feeling like you're coming out on top of the situation, and the next moment feels like you're in the bottom of a hole. Yet you must endure every step of this up and down process in order to reach the completion of your healing. As Christians, we make our biggest mistakes by feeling that we have to play the tough and conquering role before people. We're afraid to let them know we're hurting for fear of being labeled as weak or melancholy. No I'm not encouraging a pity party, but be honest with yourself. There will be times you will need to get alone and allow yourself to feel the pain that's threatening to swallow you up. Let the tears flow; tears are a part of the process. No, you can't share your pain with any and everybody, but I challenge you to sit there when you can't think of any fancy prayers and just be honest with God and yourself and just plainly state to Him what you're feeling and how helpless you seem. Sure, He already knows what you're going through, but it will make you feel better just to be able to talk to Him about it. God understands our weaknesses. Nothing better explains this than the words He spoke to the Apostle Paul in II Corinthians 12:9, "for my strength is made perfect in weakness." As human beings we put too much trust in the arms of flesh. So often we look for that loved one or best friend to help us through these difficult times, only to be disappointed time and time again when they don't come through for us. What we fail to realize is that people's "shoulders to lean on" have limitations. Sometimes depending on what you're going through or dealing with, people don't always know how to meet your needs. As humans most of us are quick to shut out what we don't understand. In previous chapters I mentioned how my sisters shunned me when I felt I needed them most. What seemed like the bad side to that, was that their rejection of me caused my pain to deepen. The flip side of that was that I learned not to depend on the arms of flesh for encouragement and comfort. Things I felt I needed to share with my family, I learned how to share with God. Many late nights leading up to the wee hours of the morning I would sit flat on the floor with tears streaming down my face and tell God my feelings, thoughts and confusions. Sometimes just to talk about what I was feeling seemed to cause my pain to intensify. And yes, I must be honest with you, there were times the prayers seem to be null and void, but I was persistent. No I didn't get immediate results, but I learned patience through tribulations. So many times I would sit or kneel to pray only to discover I couldn't figure out what words to say. I would sit there feeling like I was about to lose my mind. I had no answers and my life didn't seem to make sense any more. I went from an inspiring evangelist to a confused soul. The bottom line is I was wondering, what in the hell is going on? The more I prayed the more feelings of bitterness, anger, frustration and confusion would reveal themselves. This only confused me more; I thought when I prayed things would start to get better, not worse. Where were all these negative emotions coming from? I was grieving, grieving over the death of my mother and the rude awakening her death brought to the reality of my own life. And yet I didn't really know how to grieve.

Painfully I learned that there is a process of grieving that must be allowed to take place before we can heal properly. Most Christians have been taught the "tough mentality," such as enduring trials as a good soldier. We relate that to the scripture where the Apostle Paul was admonishing Timothy to be strong in the faith by stating; "Thou therefore endure hardness, as a soldier of Jesus Christ." II Timothy 2:3. We're often told we're not suppose to weep as those that have no hope according to the word written in I Thessalonians 4:13. In this passage of scripture Paul was addressing the church of Thessalonica in regards to the death of the saints (church members). Yet the Bible clearly states there is a time and season for all things, Ecclesiastes 3:4, a time to weep, and a time to laugh; a time to mourn and a time to dance. When God's servant Moses died, (Deuteronomy 34:8) the children of Israel wept and mourn for thirty days. God understands our tears.

Once I learned to allow myself to grieve I began to take all the pain and hurt and gear it into a positive direction. I allowed myself a time and place to cry and in the midst of those tears I would encourage myself through scriptures, prayers and songs to move forward. I stopped waiting for others to put a stamp of approval upon my life. I stopped waiting for the church officials to tell me when God had forgiven me. I sought on my own to know God's existence and will in my life. I held fast to every encouraging word I could remember through poems, sermons, famous quotes or songs. I fought daily to encourage myself some way and somehow. It was definitely a struggle but I fought to stay on top. Sometimes the pain would cause me to have a shortness of breath, yet I fought consistently just for the sake of living. Searching deep down within I began to focus on the many talents and abilities I possessed. I sought ways to put them to use through my job, my church, and my personal life. I worked hard to stay busy and focused. Still there were those moments I felt an overwhelming urge to cry. No longer would I suppress these moments unless necessary, instead I would get alone and allow myself to share those tears until I felt a relief.

Another critical part of my healing was to get away from those that were contributing to my pain, which in my case happened to be my family. It wasn't an easy task or decision but it was vital to my survival. More than anything I needed a fresh start and new surroundings. I needed to learn to believe in myself instead of what others believed for or about me. Although my moving away created a greater distance between my family and myself, it taught me strength. Not that I didn't love them any more, but I learned to love them at a distance. Sometimes it has to be this way. Perfect example; Genesis 37:28 when God allowed Joseph's brethren to sell him off to the Ishmaelites in order to fulfill his destiny. I had to stand on my own feet and learn how to fight to become the woman I was destined to be.

From the moment I moved on my own and stepped out on faith, slowly but surely my life began to fall into place. I felt as if I had stepped into a whole new world, which was frightening, challenging, and refreshing, and by the grace of God, I'm surviving. I was determined not to look back. With unshakable faith I knew that if I kept my faith and trust in God he wouldn't let me down. From that moment on I began to walk with my head up as a constant reminder to look towards the hills from whence cometh my help.

I knew when the healing began to take place; not only did I feel different about myself, but I felt different towards others. I learned to love and forgive those who hurt me, as well as forgive myself. At the same time I had to let go of all the guilt. Guilt can be very destructive and a great hindrance to your healing process. It doesn't' matter who placed the burden upon you; unless it is removed, you cannot move forward. The scripture that helped me through those guilty moments is the entire 51st chapter of Psalm when David admits his faults and failures before God and then proceeds to ask for mercy. We all make a mess of our lives every now and then but we don't have to wallow in it. For the Bible declares "For all have sinned and come short of the glory of God" (Romans 3:23).

Keeping this thought in mind I press forward. Perhaps I'll always have some wounds and emotional scars, but I'll use them as stepping stones not stumbling blocks. For I've learned that the greatest part of my healing was when I reached out to help others; that is a healing potion within itself. And so my final word to you as the reader, is that although we may have to leave a loved one, family, friends, homes, jobs, churches, and even cities or states, whatever you do don't leave God. He's the healer of lives and mender of broken hearts!

Mary F. Smith is a traveling evangelist and motivational speaker. She's also a spirituality instructor at one of the rehabilitation centers in Chicago, for pregnant women recuperating from drug and alcohol abuse.

Mary's ministry focuses on the positive aspects of life from the natural to the spiritual. Challenging women and young girls, men, and boys, to be the best of what God made you to be. She has inspired many through her ministry of, preaching, singing and dancing in the spirit.

In the face of adversity she dares to stand and tell the world, *"God always got somebody!"*

To inquire about speaking and workshop engagements contact the author at:

Mary F. Smith
P.O Box 20674
Chicago IL 60620
PH-773-994-6371

About the Author

MARY F. SMITH, multi-talented singer, poet, script and song writer, radio personality and producer for Chicago's Emmy award winning gospel music program *Testify!* Smith is the coordinator and founder of the Save the Children Youth Ministries and former Junior Pastor of the Miracle Center Church of Chicago. She is the mother of four children, and she continues to spread the gospel through ministry and song.

Smith wrote this book to encourage, inspire and enlighten others who have suffered and endured hardships. Deliverance will come. Smith believes this book will help people who are like her former self to transfer their greatest trial to their greatest testimony. Mary requests your prayers as she continues the work she was destined to do.

www.ingramcontent.com/pod-product-compliance
Lightning Source LLC
Chambersburg PA
CBHW050357290526
45786CB00003B/1019